Building Community
in an Alternative School

Studies in the
Postmodern Theory of Education

Joe L. Kincheloe and Shirley R. Steinberg
General Editors

Vol. 309

PETER LANG
New York • Washington, D.C./Baltimore • Bern
Frankfurt am Main • Berlin • Brussels • Vienna • Oxford

Lionel H. Brown & Kelvin S. Beckett

Building Community in an Alternative School

*The Perspective of an
African American Principal*

PETER LANG
New York • Washington, D.C./Baltimore • Bern
Frankfurt am Main • Berlin • Brussels • Vienna • Oxford

Library of Congress Cataloging-in-Publication Data
Brown, Lionel H.
Building community in an alternative school: the perspective
of an African American principal / Lionel H. Brown, Kelvin S. Beckett.
p. cm. — (Counterpoints: studies in the postmodern theory of education; vol. 309)
Includes bibliographical references.
1. Alternative schools—United States. 2. School improvement programs—United States.
3. Educational innovations—United States. I. Beckett, Kelvin S. II. Title.
LC46.4.B76 371.04—dc22 2007019776
ISBN 978-0-8204-8654-3
ISSN 1058-1634

Bibliographic information published by **Die Deutsche Bibliothek**.
Die Deutsche Bibliothek lists this publication in the "Deutsche
Nationalbibliografie"; detailed bibliographic data is available
on the Internet at http://dnb.ddb.de/.

Cover design by Joshua Hanson

The paper in this book meets the guidelines for permanence and durability
of the Committee on Production Guidelines for Book Longevity
of the Council of Library Resources.

© 2007 Peter Lang Publishing, Inc., New York
29 Broadway, 18th floor, New York, NY 10006
www.peterlang.com

All rights reserved.
Reprint or reproduction, even partially, in all forms such as microfilm,
xerography, microfiche, microcard, and offset strictly prohibited.

Printed in the United States of America

Contents

Preface vii

1. Alternative Schools: Portraits in Black and White 1

2. At-Risk Students: Class, Ethnicity, and Gender 17

3. Students Placed at Risk: Classroom Routines, School Rules, and
   Alienated Youth 35

4. Parent Involvement: Support or Partnership? 51

5. Separate African American Schools: Giving Voice to Silenced
   Communities 67

6. Black and White in Cincinnati: Integrated or Quality Education? 81

7. Project Succeed Academy: An Alternative School Community 95

8. Project Succeed Academy: A School/Family/Community Partnership . 113

9. White Teachers and Black Preachers: An Alliance Made in Heaven? .. 125

10. Conclusion 139

References... 145

Preface

JOHN DEWEY (1916/1944) believed that "there is more than a verbal tie between the words common, community, and communication" (p. 4). For Dewey, humans "live in a community in virtue of the things which they have in common; and communication is the way in which they come to possess things in common" (p. 4). Today, even as urban school districts strive to accommodate increasingly diverse linguistic populations, they still have difficulty serving older ethnic and socioeconomic groups. From a Deweyan perspective, for example, research on parent involvement in education indicates that urban schools are not public institutions which disadvantaged African American families and middle-class White families possess in common. Not only are middle-class White families more involved in schools than disadvantaged African American families; they are also perceived to be involved in more positive ways. Building stronger home–school communities in urban districts has been shown to have positive effects on student behavior and academic achievement (Sheldon & Epstein, 2002). But if Dewey is correct and communication is the way schools come to be possessed in common, an important measure of educational leadership in urban school districts is the ability of principals to facilitate communication and mediate disagreements between different ethnic and socioeconomic groups.

This case study contributes to a small but growing literature on alternative schools for students at risk of educational failure. Previous studies, which have focused on high schools and continuation schools, have consistently shown that alternative schools for at-risk students fail to achieve their stated aim of returning students to regular schools better equipped for academic success (Raywid, 1994b). The results of these studies can be so discouraging that readers will be forgiven if they come to think there is little school districts can do for at-risk students except warehouse them in alternative programs until they leave the school system entirely (Dunbar, 1999). The present study focuses on an alternative school for chronically disruptive elementary and middle school students in a mid-sized urban school district in the Midwest. The study is intended to show that the true mission of alternative schools is to provide a different educational environment for students whose regular schools have failed them and that alternative schools can act as a form of educational experiment to show regular schools how they can succeed with at-risk students in the future.

This study also contributes to a small but growing literature on African American educational leadership. Previous studies have shown that Black principals, building on a tradition in separate Black education whereby strong school–family–community relations were essential for the survival of their schools, understand the predominantly disadvantaged African American families they serve and communicate well with them (Lomotey, 1989). The danger of this analysis is that it leaves open the question of whether Black principals understand and communicate well with other ethnic, socioeconomic, and linguistic groups. This book shows how the Black principal of an alternative school was able to build on a second tradition in separate Black education whereby Black principals took the lead in mediating between separate Black communities and local White power structures. The principal facilitated communication and mediated disagreements between the school's main socioeconomic and ethnic communities and between the school and the larger community, and together they were able to develop policies and programs that helped all students significantly improve their behavior and academic achievement. This work has had a positive effect on district-wide policies and programs that persists even now the alternative school has been closed and its educational experiment has come to an end.

Barriers to communication across ethnic and socioeconomic lines in urban schools are being erected in an atmosphere of mutual defensiveness and distrust between increasing numbers of middle-class White teachers and increasing numbers of disadvantaged African American students and their parents (Cooper & Jordan, 2003; Miretzky, 2004). Many Black parents believe that teachers blame them for their children's discipline problems and poor academic performance and that their children's failure in school reflects badly on them as African Americans. At the same time, White teachers fear that parents hold them responsible for their children's failure and that their inability to discipline and motivate disadvantaged Black students may reflect a deep-seated, unconscious racism. Furthermore, research has shown that urban schools could do more to create opportunities for extended, meaningful, and positive communications between teachers and disadvantaged parents (Fields-Smith, 2005; Sheldon & Epstein, 2002). The only opportunities generally available now are short parent–teacher conferences and special meetings set up when a child is having academic or behavioral problems; in

Preface

both cases teachers and parents have little difficulty maintaining existing barriers to meaningful communication.

An opportunity to overcome barriers to communication across ethnic and socioeconomic lines occurred in Cincinnati in the 1990s when dramatic increases in student suspension and expulsion rates led to a city-wide focus on discipline in the public schools. Cincinnati Public Schools (CPS) student suspensions increased from 9,591 in 1990 to 20,600 in 1992, and new state regulations allowed Ohio districts to remove students from school for up to 80 days at a time (Brown, 2004). CPS was facing what was widely perceived to be a crisis in student discipline, and the response within the school system and in the city as a whole to the district's efforts to resolve the crisis was overwhelmingly negative: a broad-based community review sponsored by the CPS office of student discipline found discipline problems to be a major contributor to the district's poor student attendance record and high drop-out rate (1992); an "inventory" of the school district conducted by local business leaders was highly critical of CPS disciplinary policies (1992); a mayor's summit on education, discipline, and truancy strongly recommended that the district find ways other than suspension and expulsion to address the needs of disruptive students (1992); an external assessment by Junious Williams found that student suspensions and expulsions were too high (1993); and the Cincinnati Federation of Teachers adopted a policy of zero tolerance of student misconduct: infractions not handled properly were to be reported to the union representative for follow-up with the principal (1993).

Nor did the criticism end there. The issue of student discipline was complicated by the fact that in Cincinnati, as in other urban districts, African American students were being suspended and expelled at twice the rate of White students (Brown, 1992), and the response in the city's Black community to the district's efforts to implement race-neutral disciplinary policies was also negative: lawyers for the National Association for the Advancement of Colored People (NAACP) convinced a federal court judge that CPS was not in compliance with the terms of a school desegregation agreement, in large part because its efforts to ensure race-neutral disciplinary practices were insufficient (1991); external evaluator Junious Williams found that the school district was more effective in dealing with the discipline problems of White students than those of Black students (1993); and, in protest at the district's high rates of suspension and expulsion among African American students, a group of inner-city Black ministers campaigned successfully against a proposed school tax levy (1993).

During this period, the lead author of this book was the CPS deputy superintendent. His roles included director of the district's office of student discipline, internal compliance officer for the school desegregation agreement, and director of an alternative program for students at risk of educational failure. In reflecting on his years of service at the district level and trying to give voice to what he experienced, the lead author came to see that the main challenge he faced was to bring together concerned individuals and groups to develop consensus on new district-wide policies and programs in the area of student discipline. He was particularly concerned to facilitate dialogue and mediate disagreements between the predominantly White teachers federation and the Black ministers and between African American parent groups and the majority-White school board. The aim of these dialogues was to clarify differences in approach to student discipline, assess strengths and weaknesses, canvass alternatives, and finally work together to build consensus on new disciplinary policies and programs which would have the support of everyone.

This effort was successful (Brown & Beckett, 2006; Erkins, 2002). Agreement was first reached on the need for a new alternative school for chronically disruptive elementary and middle school students which would be free to develop discipline policies and programs appropriate for the students and families it served. Agreement was then reached on the need for a new district-wide code of student behavior which would provide a general framework within which individual schools could develop policies and programs appropriate for their communities. Schools with large numbers of at-risk students would receive district support for learning centers based on the alternative school model. Within two years of implementing these agreements, with a new alternative school serving more than 400 chronically disruptive elementary and middle school students and a new district-wide code of student behavior emphasizing the importance of pre-suspension programs for at-risk students, district suspensions and expulsions had been significantly reduced, especially among African American students, and the school district was found to be in compliance with the school desegregation agreement.

The purpose of this case study is to show how an urban school district was able to overcome barriers to communication across ethnic and socioeconomic lines and build consensus on issues relating to student discipline. The story is told from the perspective of a key participant and relies on his observation notes and journals, informal interviews with other key participants, minutes from meetings, school and school district records, contemporary newspaper reports, previous academic studies of Cincinnati's public schools, and three unpublished University of Cincinnati doctoral dissertations. The study is guided by Dewey's (1916/1944) notions of community and communication. It uses analytical tools developed by critical race theorists in education and recent research by historians of separate Black education to improve our current understanding of African American school leadership. The study shows how a Black principal was able to work with others to build a stronger school community based on policies and programs everyone could support. The study also uses recent research on alternative schools to improve our understanding of remedial programs for at-risk elementary and middle school students. It shows how an alternative school in the Midwest provided a different educational environment for chronically disruptive students whose regular schools had failed them and acted as a form of educational experiment to show regular schools how they could succeed with at-risk students in the future. The study hopes to encourage those who study urban education to investigate further the role of school and district leaders, regardless of ethnic, socioeconomic, or linguistic background, in facilitating communication and building community in today's urban schools.

Chapter 1

Alternative Schools: Portraits in Black and White

Introduction

NOWHERE is there a greater need to build stronger school communities than in alternative schools for students at risk of educational failure. Typically enrolling under-achieving and disruptive students, sometimes staffed by poorly performing and verbally abusive teachers, resented by parents as stigmatizing their children and isolating them from mainstream educational opportunities, and held accountable by school district officials if students' behavior does not improve when they return to their regular schools—alternative schools for at-risk students seem to merit their reputation as dumping grounds for students unable to succeed in regular schools. Some scholars have concluded on the basis of the available evidence that the purpose of alternative schools is not to serve the educational, social, and personal needs of at-risk students, as is declared in their mission statements, but to make regular schools safer and more conducive to learning for the majority of students by removing disruptive students from instruction and warehousing them in separate facilities.

There are two reasons we should be skeptical of this view of alternative schools for at-risk students. First, it is a perspective commonly held by students who may look down on (and fear) at-risk students, by teachers who have no direct contact with alternative schools, by parents whose only contact with the schools may be to attend entrance and exit meetings, and by school district officials whose main concern is how well at-risk students perform when they return to their regular schools. Second, it is a perspective that has yet to be tested against a substantial body of research based on first-hand observation and critical study of the alternative schools themselves. This gap in the scholarly literature is unfortunate because the past 15 years have seen a significant increase in the overall number of alternative schools, and in addition to the older "last-chance" high schools there are now more remedial elementary and middle schools whose teachers might be more committed to helping students succeed and whose parents might be more involved in their children's education. Furthermore, for all of the challenges it has faced over the past 50 years, the alternative school movement continues to thrive. Alternative schools are first and foremost educational experiments, and just as the innovations of the early suburban alternatives have led to improvements in regular high schools, the newer practices of alternative elementary and middle schools in urban districts are helping to transform the ways we approach the education of younger students. To be successful, however, these experiments must be studied and their results reported to the wider educational community. That is the purpose of this book.

Agreeing the Facts

According to the most recent statistics available, there are approximately 11,000 public alternative schools in the United States, which enroll more than 600,000 students (Kleiner, Porch, & Farris, 2002). Another recent estimate places the number of alternative schools closer to 20,000, but the authors note that what counts as an alternative varies from state to state (Lehr & Lange, 2003). Though these numbers may seem large, less than half of the public school districts in the United States have an alternative school and only 1.3% of public school students are enrolled in an alternative program. Urban school districts enrolling large numbers of low-income and ethnic minority students are more likely to have an alternative school than less diverse suburban and rural school districts. Of these urban districts, 92% enroll some of their high school students, 67% enroll some of their middle school students, and 21% enroll some of their elementary students in alternative programs. The average alternative school today enrolls approximately 60 students and has four full-time teachers on staff.

School districts report transferring students to alternative schools for a range of disciplinary offences. The most common offences are possession, distribution, or use of alcohol or drugs; fighting; chronic truancy; continual academic failure; weapons possession; and disruptive verbal behavior. Of those districts which have at least one alternative school, 86% report that they hire teachers specifically to teach in their alternative schools, 49% report that they transfer teachers by choice, and 10% report that they assign teachers involuntarily. Given the statistics available, we might imagine the typical alternative school to be urban, small, and socioeconomically and ethnically diverse and to enroll in grades 6 through 12. Though the vast majority of students have been assigned to the school as the result of a serious infraction of school rules or because they have given up trying, the teachers are at the school because that is where they want to be—they have not given up on the students.

The few large-scale studies of alternative schools undertaken to date have reported mixed results. Cox, Davidson, and Bynum (1995) conducted a meta-analytic assessment of 57 separate-curriculum, separately housed alternative school programs to determine whether the schools had positive effects on students' delinquency-related behaviors. They found that in general the alternative programs had small but significant effects on students' attitudes to school, school performance, and self-esteem but had no effect on students' delinquent behavior. More recently, as part of a study of 20 federal drop-out prevention programs, Dynarski and Gleason (2002) found that though the alternative programs studied improved student outcomes by offering smaller, more personal learning environments and additional social services, alternative middle schools in particular had difficulty maintaining enrollments because parents did not want their children involved in new and untested programs for "bad kids" and because alternative school officials, not wanting to be dumping grounds for regular schools' worst students, were especially selective in enrolling new students. Despite these mixed results, numerous case studies attest to the truth of Raywid's (1994c) view that "programs targeted for disruptive youngsters, underachievers, dropouts, and other varieties of 'at risk' youngsters have provided instances of impressive success" (p. 223) and that many of these programs have significantly improved students' self-esteem, their attitude to school, and their attendance, behavior, and academic accomplishment.

Historical Overview

Alternative schools have existed in the United States for more than 150 years (Spring, 2005). During this time, the word "alternative" has been used to describe a wide range of schools set up to offer significantly different forms of education to the education provided by most schools of the day. Catholics created the first alternatives because they perceived the mid-19th-century common schools to be dominated by Protestants, and by the end of the 19th century trade unions were sponsoring alternatives to what they thought were anti-union public school systems in urban areas. This history is explained by the fact that the earliest public school promoters were "typically British-American in origin, Protestant in religion, and entrepreneurial in economic outlook" (Tyack & Hansot, 1982, p. 21): "they were intolerant of the Roman Catholic Church and so alienated Catholics that they hastened the growth of a separate parochial-school system" (pp. 21–22), and "as citizens near the economic apex of their local communities, attuned to the values and economic interests of a burgeoning capitalism, they praised the United States as a land of economic opportunity and justice and tended to blame the poor for their plight" (p. 22). In Cincinnati, for example, Catholics mounted a campaign in the 1860s against the use of the King James version of the Bible (Tyack & Hansot, 1982). When the schools refused to allow teachers to use other versions, Catholics in the city established their own schools. A lawyer involved in the Cincinnati Bible case said that "in my judgment, the contest is not about religious education at all. It is about denominational supremacy, the right to be higher, to be better, to be more powerful than your neighbor" (cited in Tyack & Hansot, 1982, p. 22).

In the 20th century, beginning with the pre–World War I anarchist schools and continuing in larger numbers with post–World War II free schools, the dominant theme was the establishment of alternatives to what were perceived to be large, bureaucratic, authoritarian, and oppressive high schools. The free schools, which were inspired by A. S. Neil's Summerhill School in England, became the model for the first alternative schools introduced into public school systems. When graduates of one alternative high school in a large Midwestern city were asked how their school, which featured community involvement programs, differed from regular schools, the theme that emerged most strongly from what they said was freedom from oppression:

> Shawna: "we were out in the community doing our own work most of the time....Nobody here took up the school space as if it was theirs and not yours. It was everyone's place." (Swaminathan, 2004, p. 53)

> Marie (on college track in regular school; gets pregnant): "it was as if no one could see me any more....I was fading out of school....They expected me to dropout and never finish school." (p. 49)

> Jason: "the placements helped a lot....I went to parts of this city that I had never been to before. I used to hardly ever leave my neighborhood." (p. 55)
>
> Todd: "there are all these stupid rules—that's why I really like Parkside, man—I finally felt like an adult. Here I was, living on my own, looking after my grandma and I am not allowed to go outside for lunch." (p. 50)
>
> Lisa: "I found out I had a father who was alive and didn't know I existed. That's when I guess I stayed out of school—to think about stuff. I met him and worked out my personal life a bit." (p. 46)

In public school systems today, magnet schools are intended to offer parents "quality" alternatives to low-achieving neighborhood schools. Magnet schools were first established in the 1970s as part of voluntary desegregation agreements that school districts were reaching with the National Association for the Advancement of Colored People (NAACP) and other individuals and groups representing African American students and their families. In the place of forced busing to predominantly White schools, new schools with specialized curriculums or teaching methods would act as magnets to attract students from throughout the district and would be required to maintain racial balance. As one historian has said, "[B]y the early 1980s, the variety of choices available to students in some school systems would have astounded educators in the early part of the century" (Spring, 1994, p. 356). In Cincinnati, where the public school system reached an agreement with the NAACP in 1984 on a desegregation plan that relied solely on magnet schools, "alternatives" (as they are known locally) flourished. By the early 1990s the Cincinnati Public Schools had schools specializing in creative and performing arts, athletics, languages, science and mathematics, computer sciences, and college preparation, making its magnet school program proportionately one of the largest in the country (Taylor & Yu, 1999).

Drawing Distinctions

Raywid (1993, 1994b) distinguishes three main types of public alternative school programs: popular innovation programs, last-chance programs, and remedial programs. The significant contrast is between older, less expensive, and more successful popular innovation programs, which have their roots in the free schools of the 1970s and serve mainly middle-class White high school students in the suburbs, and newer, more expensive, and less successful last-chance and remedial programs, which trace their history to pre–

World War II continuation schools and serve mainly low-income and ethnic and linguistic minority middle school and high school students in the cities. Though last-chance and remedial programs feature smaller class sizes and more social services than popular innovation programs, research has shown that enrollment in these programs results in only temporary improvements in student behavior and academic achievement. One alternative school administrator draws the contrast in striking terms when he compares the "idealistic havens" of the 1970s, which welcomed students who were "turned off" and "tuned out" in their regular schools, with alternative schools today, to which "disruptive, deviant, and dysfunctional" students have been sent to protect students at regular schools (McGee, 2001). The administrator goes on to tell the story of how he invited student journalists from the local high school to visit his school and interact with his students, and of how they entered the school with fear and trepidation—afraid that it might be "a 'Dangerous Minds' school full of druggies and gang members" (p. 589)—and left at the end of the day with a very positive impression: "I felt more comfortable among Hamilton students than I do among teens I go to school with" (p. 590).

Popular Innovation Programs

We have already noted that popular innovation programs were originally inspired by independent free schools based on the educational philosophy of A. S. Neil. Popular innovation programs are intended to make schooling more challenging and fulfilling for mainly suburban and small-town high school students who feel alienated in larger, more bureaucratic regular schools. Popular innovation schools are politically viable because of their popularity with some parents and because, by maintaining existing student–teacher ratios, the cost per student is roughly the same as in regular schools. Their success is based on their ability to offer a coherent alternative to regular school programs, to recruit dedicated teachers, and to enroll students who are wiling to take responsibility for their education.

Gold and Mann (1984) conducted an early study of three alternative education programs in Michigan. Each program served 30–60 predominantly White, working- and middle-class, grades 7–12 students in suburban school districts. The researchers describe students' disruptive and delinquent behavior as a form of rebellion against standards of success in their regular schools which resulted in a poor self-image and low self-esteem. They contrast rigid role regulation of social relations in the students' regular schools, which separated students from teachers, with warm, accepting relationships with teachers in the alternative schools and conclude that these relationships provided a check against impulses to disruptive behavior. The researchers also describe rigid rule enforcement in the students' regular schools and contrast it with the relative freedom students enjoyed in their alternative schools. One boy, talking about gym class in his regular school, said, "If you don't get dressed, you get an E for that day. What if you forgot your gym shoes? How can you get dressed?" (p. 107). In the boy's alternative school, on the other hand, we are told that students come and go freely, that noise levels are occasionally higher, and that space is provided for coffee and a smoke.

Popular innovation programs now also serve predominantly low-income, ethnic minority students in large urban school districts. Raywid (1994a) describes a laboratory school in New York which serves 100 grades 10–12 students, most of whom "share...a past that has included difficulties in accepting and dealing with school authority" (p. 94). Students and teachers work together on a demanding inquiry-based curriculum which features projects on topics of concern to urban students and issues students find genuinely challenging. Though students' SAT scores range from 400 to 1,400, in the eight years of the school's existence no student has dropped out and 95% of graduates have entered college. Raywid (1994a) also notes that "[f]ew disciplinary problems arise, and virtually none of a confrontational, showdown nature have occurred. The school's sole absolute rule of 'no fighting' has never been violated in its eight years, and on the sole occasion when that record was threatened, it was students who stepped in to uphold it" (p. 105).

Last-chance Programs

Last-chance programs trace their history to continuation schools established in the 1920s to serve as a bridge between school and work for working-class and immigrant boys and as a preparation for household service and marriage for pregnant or mothering girls. In the 1950s and 1960s many of these programs were re-focused to re-direct academic non-achievers, discipline cases, truants, and juvenile delinquents "back into the regular full time school program with a much better understanding of the requirements of society" (Kelly, 1993, p. 51). Today last-chance programs mainly serve disadvantaged high school students in urban districts who have been expelled from regular schools for severely disruptive behavior. Though many still prepare students to return to their regular schools, some now offer their own degrees. Last-chance programs are politically viable because, even though they are unpopular with some parents and have low student–teacher ratios and additional social services, school districts can justify the increased cost per student by pointing to the benefits that accrue to the vast majority of students in regular schools when severely disruptive students are removed from instruction.

The curricular focus at last-chance schools may have changed over the years, but the purpose is still to provide students with a bridge to the adult world. Wonalancet Alternative School in New Hampshire, for example, offers an outdoor education program that features activities, such as climbing and rappelling, that test students' ability to work together in groups; conservation opportunities such as building nature trails, improving wildlife habitats, and removing eyesores; and peer tutoring in elementary schools and helping out at a local nursing home (Goodman, 1999). The Center for Alternative Learning in Tennessee, to take a second example, has adopted a "one-room schoolhouse" concept in which each teacher is assigned a qualified counselor and a teaching assistant and is encouraged to develop a unique learning environment and nurturing family atmosphere playing to his or her individual strengths. Students are then assigned to the classroom that best fits their individual needs (Kennedy & Morton, 1999).

Remedial Programs

Remedial programs, which are the focus of the present study, are the newest and least studied form of alternative public school program. Remedial programs serve mainly disadvantaged elementary and middle school students in urban districts who need more academic, social, and personal support than regular schools can provide (Raywid, 1994b, 1995). Like last-chance programs, remedial schools feature small class sizes and additional social services. Unlike last-chance programs, however, they typically enroll younger students and "attempt to generate the conditions that will stimulate social and emotional growth—a matter often seen as calling for a focus on the school as community" (Raywid, 1995, pp. 125–126). Thus, "the environments they provide are typically small, supportive, and have positive student-adult relationships, and considerable amounts of individual attention" (p. 128).

Remedial schools have yet to prove they are politically viable. Though student behavior and academic achievement often improve in remedial schools, these improvements are not sustained when students return to their regular schools. As a result, school districts "typically conclude that the programs have failed to bring about the improvements sought—rarely, if ever, that the students involved can succeed in an alternative school environment. Thus evidence that supports the need for such variants is often read as testimony to their failure" (Raywid, 1995, pp. 128–129). We argue that the present study of a remedial school for elementary and middle school students in the Midwest supports Raywid's (1995) contention that it is only by establishing remedial schools on a permanent basis that urban school districts can serve the needs of students who are most at risk for educational failure.

Clarifying the Issues

The authors of a recent report from the Alternative School Research Project at the University of Minnesota note that though alternative programs were "innovative" and "progressive" in the 1960s and 1970s, they "became more conservative and remedial in the 1980s and began serving more students who were disruptive or failing in their home schools" (Lehr & Lange, 2003, p. 61). Today, alternative programs for at-risk students are widely perceived to include students who behave badly, teachers who do not care, parents who are not involved, and school district officials who are not supportive. They are no longer intended to provide innovative and progressive school environments for students whose needs are not being met in regular schools; instead, the true purpose of alternative programs today is thought to be to improve the educational environments of students who are not at risk of educational failure by removing disruptive students from regular schools and warehousing them in separate facilities.

These views can be found in the reports of two recent studies of alternative school programs serving mainly disadvantaged African American youth. Dunbar (1999, 2001) conducted an in-depth study of an alternative program for at-risk high school students in the Midwest. On the basis of this study, studies by other researchers, and his experience as an alternative school teacher, Dunbar concludes that "the major push behind alternative school policies (for this population) is to remove students from the traditional school in order to make the school safe for other students" (2001, p. 120). Similarly, when Carpenter-Aeby and Aeby (2001) began a study of an alternative program for middle school and high school students in the southeast, they found that the original purpose of the program when it was established in the 1970s was "to create safer schools by simply removing disruptive students without any intervention" (p. 78).

But even if we restrict ourselves to considering the limited evidence available in the research literature, there is reason to doubt that the picture painted so far is the whole picture. As we will see in the following chapters, the newer alternative schools, however "conservative" and "remedial" they may appear, also make serious efforts to serve the needs of their students, and with the help of dedicated teachers, involved parents, and supportive school district officials, many at-risk students are provided with more appropriate forms of education in environments more conducive to learning than in their regular schools. Even Carpenter-Aeby and Aeby (2001) found that the school they studied had changed dramatically during the 1990s, introducing smaller classes and additional social services, and making serious efforts to get the parents and guardians of at-risk students more involved in their children's education.

Students Who Behave Badly?

Raywid (1993) reminds us that though last chance alternative programs are "designed for the worst of students. They have aptly been called 'soft jails' since their students typically are 'sentenced' to them, often as one final opportunity before expulsion" (p. 25), remedial programs are non-punitive, being "designed for youngsters presenting special needs—for example students requiring remediation, or in emotional difficulty" (p. 26). But Raywid goes on to say that the youngsters involved in remedial programs have often "accepted the perception that they are losers and internalized the message....This may actually stimulate the forging of strong bonds between them—but it also disposes them to see themselves as a community of losers and one denigrated by others" (pp. 26–27). The danger is that students who see themselves as "losers" will act accordingly. Like the students in Dunbar's (1999) study of a last-chance high school,

> Once warehoused, the students adopt those roles most functional for the setting. ... Most of the students I observed exhibited inappropriate behavior in part because enrollment in this school was a license to behave disruptively. Acceptable behavior was the exception not the rule....Doors slamming, altercations, loud voices, and verbal abuse could be heard anytime during the course of the day....Far removed from sites where status can be attained through a variety of positive means (good grades, sports), these students worked to outdo themselves by being "bad," wearing inappropriate behaviors like badges of honor. (p. 3)

Students are enrolled in remedial programs as a result of behavioral problems associated with emotional difficulties or because of academic problems that require remediation. Remedial programs are premised on the belief that if a program succeeds in addressing students' behavioral and academic problems the students will come to see themselves as winners and act accordingly. So how do alternative education students see themselves? According to one recent large-scale study, students enrolled in alternative programs see themselves in much the same way as other students see themselves. Wiest, Wong, Cervantes, and Kreil (2001) studied intrinsic motivation among regular, special, and alternative education high school students in a large, ethnically diverse Southern California school district. Even though the GPAs of the alternative students were significantly lower than those of the regular and special education students, and even though they rated their academic ability somewhat lower than did the other two groups, there was no statistically significant difference in self-perceived social competence or self-esteem. The researchers concluded:

> Students with chronic difficulties in school may in fact assess themselves as deficient in the domain of academic competence without injuring their overall sense of self-efficacy. This is quite striking, since so much of adolescent life is organized around school. Nevertheless, their inner life may be organized in a much broader manner, such that academic success is not as dominant as would be expected. (pp. 122–123)

Teachers Who Don't Care?

Dunbar (1999) observes that "when students in alternative schools complain, 'This school is dumb' or 'We don't learn nothing here,' they express an understanding that they are not participating in a legitimate academic education" (p. 6). The reason, according to Raywid (1993), is that it is not just alternative school students who tend to see themselves as losers: "alternative school faculties are inclined to see their charges this way too" (p. 27), and "if it is assumed that the problems lie within the students, then changes in school organization and program and practice are not the solution and probably can't matter very much" (p. 27). In remedial programs teachers "are likely to see their charges as weaker than other students in some important way and as needing more help and direction than other youngsters" (p. 27): "However sympathetic and compassionate they may be, their gestalt tends to be professional, rather than communal. It assumes that they, the teachers, remain primarily the professionals engineering the development of their students, rather than first and foremost human beings accompanying and guiding the young in their progress toward competent maturity" (p. 27). For Raywid, this gestalt in many remedial programs "leaves intact a dominant adult or 'official' school culture on the one hand, and a separate student subculture on the other" (p. 28).

In many alternative programs, however, teachers know they can make a difference and they strive to develop a communal atmosphere on the basis of personal bonds with their students. These bonds may be based on shared personal experience. Goodman (1999), for example, tells us that when he was a student he was suspended and expelled for disruptive behavior. He knows "oppositional" students because he was one himself. When his students say a field trip sucks he pretends to think they are saying the trip is fantastic, and when they say, no, they really mean it sucks, he asks them to find a new word to express their opinion. Subsequently, the students learn to say that bad field trips are awesome, and when they say that good field trips suck, they say it with a smile. And then there is his "fuck lecture." Goodman tells his students that "fuck" is his favorite word but they are ruining it for him by using it all the time. They should save it for important occasions, such as when a canoe falls on their feet. After listening to his fuck lecture, the students stare momentarily, mouths agape, and then say, "That's cool."

The basis of the bond between alternative education teachers and students, however, is more often an attempt by teachers to create a caring, family atmosphere at school that many students do not have at home. Kennedy and Morton (1999), for example, give an account of an alternative learning center for middle school and high school students in a mid-sized Tennessee city which the authors describe as a school for emotional healing. When students misbehave, Morton, the director of the school, responds by explaining to the students the consequences of their misbehavior for everyone at the school, says that as director of the school he is responsible for these consequences, and then asks the students to share his responsibility by exploring the misbehavior with him to discover its root causes. As a result of this approach, students find that "the cause of their troubles was not in their intentions but in the mistakes they made in interpreting the facts of some situations or in the strategies they chose to use to correct injustices they encountered" (p. vii). The implicit message to students is that they are not just individuals responding to what they perceive to be mistreatment by teachers or other students but also members of a family with responsibilities to other members. Students respond when they realize that the center is "home" and that others care for them and want them to do well.

Finally, the basis of the bond between alternative school teachers and students may be cultural. Murrell (2002), for example, in his account of African-centered schools, says that in the early years of African experience in America "education was viewed as the result of guided participation in the doings of the community by elders" (p. 31). This perspective is still common today:

> There are many "in the flow" occasions where the teacher uses language to reorient behavior: "Please take out your journals....Mailik, what did I just say?" Culturally mainstream teachers are trained to think of this as discipline....This is a different perspective from that of accomplished practice among urban African American teachers....This is merely a condition in which the young person is in "need of assistance" to get them back on track, easily provided by the power of the word. (p. 133)

Like the students at the learning center in Tennessee, students at African-centered schools are encouraged to see themselves as belonging to the same community as their elders and as needing assistance from elders when learning how members of the community behave.

Parents Who are Not Involved?

Until recently, the vast majority of alternative schools served high school students. In most case studies of these schools the topic of parent involvement does not arise. Dunbar (1999), for example, mentions parents only once, and that is to describe their opposition to alternative programs. Writing of a public meeting on a government bill relating to alternative schools for disruptive students in Illinois, he says that parents "were vehemently opposed to the bill and expressed concern about the labeling and subsequent isolation of their children from mainstream educational opportunities" (p. 3).

It is only in the past 20 years that school districts have begun experimenting with alternative forms of education for elementary and middle school students. In the few case studies of alternative elementary and middle school programs published to date, parent involvement appears to be minimal. In one study of a grades 4–12 school, for example, what is described as "extensive" parent involvement seems to amount to little more than attending entrance, progress, and exit meetings and receiving family-focused social services (Aeby, Manning, Thyer, & Carpenter-Aeby, 1999; Carpenter-Aeby & Aeby, 2001).

There is a second reason for the lack of parent involvement in alternative education programs regardless of the age of the students, and this goes to the root cause of the disruptive behavior that brings students to alternative schools in the first place. Wiest, Wong, Cervantes, and Kreil (2001), in their large-scale study of intrinsic motivation among regular, special, and alternative education high school students in Southern California, say:

> A clear finding was the perception by alternative education students that their parents were less involved in their lives and less supportive. These students rated their parents as less likely to listen, understand problems, ask about school, or talk to teachers. Their parents were also considered to be more punitive and authoritarian. In short, these parents were characterized as relating to their children in extremes, being either unavailable or controlling. (p. 123)

We should not be surprised that the parents of many alternative school students are not available for them at school: they appear not to be available for them at home either.

School Districts Which Are Not Supportive?

We have seen that school districts are typically slow to respond to the needs of at-risk students, that they make a minimal commitment when they do respond, and that they are quick to declare alternative programs for at-risk students to have failed when students' behavior and academic achievement do not improve when they return to their regular schools. One alternative school, for example, was originally established to create safer regular schools by removing their most disruptive students and was allowed to continue as a warehouse for disruptive students for 20 years before some drop-out prevention programs and other social services were provided (Aeby, Manning, Thyer, & Carpenter-Aeby, 1999; Carpenter-Aeby & Aeby, 2001). The programs in Michigan studied by Gold and Mann (1984), to take a second example, consisted of 2 teachers, 1 aide or secretary, and 30–60 students occupying a few rooms in a wing of an unused elementary school. Finally, Wonalancet Alternative School in New Hampshire seems to have involved fewer than 20 students chosen by councilors at Wonalancet High School who had failed 9th grade and were considered disruptive (Goodman, 1999). The aim was to "reconnect" the students to Wonalancet High as quickly as possible and to have them graduate there.

Another measure of commitment is the practice of many school districts of contracting with outside organizations to provide alternative programs for their most disruptive students. At Kennedy and Morton's (1999) "school for healing" in Tennessee, though each classroom had a teacher, counselor, and aide, the school itself consisted of only three classrooms run by a non-profit organization trying to serve the needs of suspended and expelled students from two school districts in a mid-sized city. Though this school appears to have been successful despite the limited commitment of the school districts it was intended to serve, the same cannot be said of "New Hope," an alternative program for 67 predominantly African American middle school students in a Midwest city (Schutz and Harris, 2001). New Hope, which is run out of a community center, is said to be in crisis: staff are unqualified and ineffectual, and turnover is high; because staff focus narrowly on their own classrooms there are no teacher-sponsors for extra activities; student attendance is declining, and when students do attend they frequently get into altercations with other students and with teachers.

Conclusion

Raywid (1995) asserts that "many of the most promising proposals for improving the education of at-risk students—as well as many of the most popular reform recommendations for the education of all students—have drawn on the practice of alternative schools" (p. 119). In support of her claim, she reminds us that "many of the reforms currently pursued in traditional schools—downsizing the high school, pursuing a focus or theme, student and teacher choice, making the school a community, empowering staff, active learner engagement, authentic assessment—are practices that alternative schools pioneered" (Raywid, 1994b, p. 26). But these are examples of reforms pioneered in popular innovation programs for suburban high school students beginning in the 1960s and 1970s. The focus of the present study is on a remedial program for urban elementary and middle school students which began in the 1990s. The question we must address is, What practices are remedial schools pioneering that traditional schools might adopt in the future?

We have seen that remedial programs for at-risk students are intended to provide small, home-like environments in which students feel cared for (Raywid, 1993, 1995) and that in successful programs students form strong bonds with their teachers and come to see themselves as winners. Case studies of these programs, however, seem to indicate that to achieve this goal, remedial schools could provide more opportunities for parents to become involved in their children's education (Carpenter-Aeby & Aeby, 2001). One of the themes that emerges from the present study is that when an alternative school develops new ways of involving parents in all aspects of their children's education, both at home and at school, and when the school is innovative in providing parents with the type of support they need to become involved in meaningful ways, increased parental involvement can make a significant contribution to creating the type of family atmosphere many alternative education students need before they can focus on learning.

We have also seen that remedial programs require support from their school districts to provide the small class sizes and additional social services that at-risk students need (Aeby, Manning, Thyer, & Carpenter-Aeby, 1999; Carpenter-Aeby & Aeby, 2001). But case studies of remedial programs indicate that school districts can do more to provide the forms of support these programs require (Schutz & Harris, 2001). A second theme that emerges from the present study is that when a school district finds new ways to support alternative forms of education for at-risk elementary and middle school students—including provision of buildings to house programs, qualified teaching staff, social services, and a full range of extra-curricular activities; in other words, when they treat alternative programs for at-risk students in the same way they have come to treat other programs for specific student populations—student behavior will improve and academic gains will be made.

Chapter 2

At-Risk Students: Class, Ethnicity, and Gender

Introduction

SCHOOL DISTRICTS transfer students to alternative schools because they have committed a serious infraction of school rules, such as weapons possession or alcohol or drug use, or because of persistent disruptive behavior, truancy, or academic failure. Typically, a single infraction will result in suspension or expulsion, and enrollment in an alternative school is reserved for repeat offenders, that is, students who continue to break the rules even after they have been suspended and expelled several times. Who are these students? Why do they persist in being disruptive? Is the explanation to be found by looking more closely at the students, their families, or their communities, or should we be examining the people, policies, and programs that make up our traditional schools? The issue we face is that there are no easy answers to these questions, but without answers of some kind we cannot respond effectively to disruptive students. In this chapter we argue that even if demographic variables clearly make some students more at risk of academic failure than others, the fact that many of these students succeed in alternative educational environments suggests that traditional schools could do more to respond to the needs of at-risk students.

Agreeing the Facts

Student discipline continues to be a major concern of the public and of parents with children in public schools (Brown & Beckett, 2006). The problem of student discipline is especially acute at a time when schools are being held more accountable for student academic success. Numerous studies have shown a direct positive correlation between student behavioral problems and academic failure, and chronically disruptive students, though only a small percentage of the school population, can have a major effect on the learning of all students. The problem of student discipline disproportionately affects urban school districts with large numbers of low-income and ethnic minority students. Research has shown that African American and Latino students and students of low socioeconomic status are punished more often and more severely than other students (Skiba, Michael, Nardo, & Peterson, 2002). For example, though African American students constitute only 17% of the nation's school population, they represent 34% of students who receive out-of-school suspensions. Studies have also shown that boys are four times more likely than girls to be referred to the office, to be suspended, and to receive corporal punishment. When ethnicity and gender are combined, it has been found that Black males are 16 times more likely than White females, and 156 times more likely than Asian females, to receive corporal punishment.

The problem of student discipline in urban schools is compounded by a widespread belief among disadvantaged students and their parents that school disciplinary policies are administered unfairly. Many studies have demonstrated that levels of disruptive behavior are higher in schools where students perceive such unfairness. Some students "interpret the disparity as rejection and as a result develop a collective self-fulfilling belief that they are incapable of abiding by schools' social and behavioral codes" (Browne, Losen, & Wald, 2002, p. 77), and others see it as a "challenge to escalate their behavior" (Skiba & Knesting, 2001, p. 33). Studies have also shown that levels of disruptive behavior are higher in urban schools serving predominantly low-income and ethnic minority families where parents are less involved in school-related activities. But one of the reasons disadvantaged parents commonly give for not being more involved in their children's schooling is their belief that teachers and administrators punish their children unfairly.

Studies have shown that student discipline is not a major issue in schools where students are fully engaged in curricular and extra-curricular activities. But studies have also shown that disadvantaged minority students are less involved than middle-class White students in the full range of educational opportunities offered by our public schools. Not only do disadvantaged minority students spend less time in school because they are suspended or expelled and drop out at higher rates than middle-class White students; they are also under-represented in high-ability classroom groupings and in gifted and advanced placement programs and over-represented in programs for students with special needs. They are also over-represented in poorly funded urban schools which offer a narrower range of curricular and extra-curricular options and which are less able to attract and retain teachers qualified in the subject areas they teach than predominantly White suburban schools (Ladson-Billings & Tate, 1995). Different levels of student involvement are also indicated by gaps in academic achievement in most subject areas. The most recent evidence on student achievement suggests that over the past 30 years African American students have closed the gap with White students but still have not achieved parity and that the gaps between poor and middle-class students remain as large as they were 30 years ago (National Center for Education Statistics, 2005).

Clarifying the Issues

Given the evidence presented here, it is tempting to conclude that poverty and minority status are sufficient explanations for academic disengagement and disruptive behavior. Poverty, after all, is associated with poor nutrition and chronic health problems, and minority status is historically related to low self-esteem, making it difficult for disadvantaged students to focus on learning. Can we not say that students at risk of educational failure are individuals whose family and community backgrounds make it difficult for them to engage with school and who as a consequence are restless and disruptive? The problem with this explanation is that it ignores some of the evidence presented. What are we to make of the fact that many disadvantaged students and their parents believe that schools administer discipline policies unfairly? It can be argued that the injustices are real, that disadvantaged students are alienated and angry, and that acting out is their way of resisting injustice. What are we to make of the fact that low-income and ethnic minority families have less access to well-funded public schools, quality educational programs, and qualified teachers? It can be argued that disadvantaged parents are also alienated and angry and that their refusal to give teachers the type of support they say they need is a form of passive resistance to injustice.

When research is presented relating student discipline and academic achievement to demographic variables, the findings represent averages. Hidden beneath the averages may be considerable variation in individual cases. Raffaele Mendez, Knoff, and Ferron (2002), for example, examined student demographic variables and out-of-school suspension rates in a large, ethnically diverse Florida school district. As we would expect, the researchers found that boys were suspended more often than girls and African American students more often than White students. But the researchers also found that within groups of demographically matched schools there was considerable variation in suspension rates. They found that schools with high suspension rates focused on punishment of inappropriate behavior, while schools with low suspension rates focused on positive reinforcement of good behaviors, on formal social skills training, and on involving parents in the development of school-wide discipline plans. These findings suggest that while poverty and minority status put students at greater risk of educational failure, school policies, programs, and personnel are also factors in determining which students succeed and which students fail. This hypothesis is confirmed by the many case studies that show that when disadvantaged students gain access to well-funded public schools where qualified teachers offer quality educational programs, the majority are successful (Brown & Beckett, 2006).

Those Black Boys

Fordham (2001) observes that in many Black communities the street is seen as masculine social space "where impoverished bodies are compelled to live and where what is constructed as the most culturally 'authentic' prevails" (p. 148). Much the same can be seen in urban schools, where poor Black male students feel compelled to create space for themselves at the backs of classrooms, in the hallways, lunchrooms, and gyms, and on the playgrounds outside, and where a separate Black male culture prevails that is both feared and envied. None of this is remarkable—after all, all youth, rich and poor, Black and White, male and female, feel the need to create space for themselves. But the notion of separate social spaces being created in urban schools brings into focus the challenges faced by poor Black male students and predominantly middle-class White female teachers when they try to create spaces they can share.

Research has shown that when Black male students are compared with other students by gender and race they consistently have the worst attendance record, rank lowest in academic achievement, are suspended and expelled the most often, and are most likely to drop out of school and fail to graduate or earn a GED (Brown, 2005). A recent study found that Cincinnati and Cleveland lead the nation in graduating the fewest Black male students: only 19% of students entering 9th grade in 1997–1998 graduated with their cohort four years later (Holzman, 2004). Recent research has also shown that poor performance at elementary and secondary school limits Black males' participation in college and in adult society generally, correlating strongly with low levels of employment and disproportionately large numbers in jails and penitentiaries. Adult Black males are also characterized as having more health problems and as dying at a younger age than any other racial or gender group in America.

How does this happen? Davis (2003) reports, "In general, African American boys have very positive experiences in early schooling. Almost all of them… report looking forward to going to kindergarten each day, and the vast majority of them like their teacher and say good things about their school" (p. 524). Throughout the primary years, however, tension builds between Black males' home culture and their school culture (Brown, 2005). Black male students may be more active than other students, may resolve conflict more often with physical contact, and may be more vocal when they believe they are treated unfairly. By the time they reach middle school, many Black male students have become apathetic, sometimes disruptive, young men. They may engage in "challenging behaviors common to the African American male adolescent community" because they consider their lessons "irrelevant, racist, or too simplistic" (Schwartz, 2001, p. 4), because they think their teachers believe them to be incapable of achieving, or because they are unable "to keep up with white classmates because of learning or developmental differences" (p. 4).

By the time Black male students reach middle school, many teachers perceive them to be undesirable elements in their classrooms and fear them as aggressive, even potentially violent (Boyd-Franklin & Franklin, 2000). Studies have shown that at this level Black students begin to be punished for more subjective reasons than White students. In a study of middle school students in a large Midwestern school district, for example, it was found that while White students were referred to the office for objective offenses such as smoking, leaving class without permission, obscene language, and vandalism, Black students were referred to the office for offenses requiring more subjective judgment such as loitering, excessive noise, disrespect, and threat (Skiba, Michael, Nardo, & Peterson, 2002). Finally, the transition to high school is especially difficult for many Black male students. In these larger, more anonymous schools, teachers may rely more on stereotypes in interpreting Black male behavior, and high school administrators are under greater pressure to emphasize discipline, including zero tolerance for membership in what are perceived to be street gangs.

Researchers have also found that the gaps between Black male students' and other students' levels of academic achievement begin to emerge only in 4th grade. Davis (2003), for example, reports that Black male students performed as well as their peers on district-wide assessments in reading and math in the 3rd grade but experienced a sharp decline in their test scores in the 4th grade. Gentry and Peelle (1994) call this "the confrontation point":

> At about third or fourth grade, when schools begin national achievement testing and have established their tracks, poor children—especially black boys—begin to get the message about their place in society. Too many of them have not been taught to read well, and they have not assimilated successfully into the school culture....Even when their early achievement is up to the level of other students, after fourth grade they fall farther and farther behind, usually entering junior high school one or two full grades behind. (p. 35)

By this time in their academic careers, even middle-class Black students begin to give up on school. Ogbu (2003) studied middle-class Black students at majority-White schools in Shaker Heights, Ohio. He found that by their middle school and high school years the efforts made by the students to succeed in their academic subjects had "decreased markedly" (p. 20) and they were following a "norm of minimum effort" (p. 23). The students told researchers that it was not "cool" to succeed in school. Some were "drifting" into nonacademic activities such as sports, believing they were going to "make it" there. For others, however, the only respect, encouragement, and sense of achievement they got was from peers outside of school, and the alliances they formed there were based in part on a shared belief that school was not important and that working for good grades was "feminine" or "acting White."

Why does this happen? For Davis (2001), "Black boys are loved and loathed at school. They are heroes and standard bearers of hip-hop culture and athleticism in schools, while simultaneously experiencing disproportionate levels of punishment and academic marginality" (p. 169). He analyses the "the cool pose hypothesis [which] suggests that young Black males adopt and display behaviors and attitudes that they think convey a sense of their coolness, esteem, and cultural attachment" but which is "misunderstood by White middle-class teachers and school administrators as defiant, aggressive, and intimidating" (p. 172). In his own study of Black male students from different socioeconomic backgrounds attending a middle school in an upper-middle-class White neighborhood in the Northeast, Davis (2001) found "a distinct black male-centered cultural space" (p. 174) with "an accepted code

At-Risk Students

of masculinized conduct" (p. 174) and "masculine presentational behavior including hallway walk, how one talks, school attire—particularly sneakers and over-sized shirts and pants, lunchroom seating patterns, and how boys carry their books and bags" (p. 177). But he also found that in the school Black males had a "marginalized...social status" (p. 175), noting, for example, that interracial dating was not acceptable.

Many researchers and writers trace the roots of conflict between Black male students and White female teachers to differences in mother–son relationships between many Black and White families. Kunjufu (1986), an African American educator, workshop presenter, and writer, has found that for many White female teachers "their black students may be the first Black males with whom they have ever had direct contact," and he wonders, "[H]ow can you teach a child whom you do not understand?" (p. 12). Kunjufu believes that many African American mothers are overly protective of their sons, explaining that Black mothers historically had to shield their sons "to keep them from being lynched" (p. 2). This belief is confirmed by several other studies. Cook and Fine (1995), for example, found that disadvantaged African American mothers living in areas with high levels of violence and crime are more protective of their sons than middle-class White mothers living in safer neighborhoods, and in a study of Black students at "Capital High" in Washington, DC, Fordham (1996) found that mothers of under-achieving male students appeared "to seek the approval of these males by not criticizing them, not setting limitations, and not demanding a relationship based on mutual respect" (p. 171).

The problem is that many Black males, knowing their mothers to be overly protective, feel they can manipulate them to get what they want and make the mistake of assuming that "the way they...manipulate their mothers can also be used with their female teachers" (Kunjufu, 1986, p. 9). Middle-class White female teachers, however, coming from a culture in which there is less of a felt need to be protective of their sons or to seek their approval, are unlikely to respond well to attempts by their Black male students to manipulate them. They may interpret Black male students' increased activity and physical contact as willful and disruptive and their protestations of unfair treatment as challenges to their authority. As Black male students grow bigger and stronger, White female teachers may begin to feel concern for their safety and to refer the students to the office more frequently and for more subjective reasons. But, to paraphrase Kunjufu, how can you teach a child whom you fear?

Those Loud Black Girls

The picture that emerges from the literature suggests that Black female students have been more successful than Black male students in creating space for themselves in urban classrooms. This is indicated by quantitative studies that show Black female students consistently outperform Black male students on achievement tests and are punished less often and less severely than Black male students. It is also indicated by several recent case studies which focus on the challenges disadvantaged Black female students face in urban schools and on the efforts they make to succeed. Lei (2003), for example, conducted a two-year ethnographic study which contrasts "loud" Black girls with "quiet" Asian boys at a high school in the Midwest. In the study, the Black girls are seen by others and by themselves as large, loud, and aggressive, blocking hallways between classes, daring other students to pass, and challenging teachers for leadership in their classrooms. For some of the teachers in the study the attitudes and behaviors associated with Black girls indicate a positive self-image, cockiness, confidence, and a refusal to back down. One teacher is quoted as saying that "if you belittle them or embarrass them, they're gonna get angry. They're *more* likely to get a little in your face than a girl who's white might" (p. 165). But some of the older girls have begun to understand that behind this tolerance is barely disguised disapproval, and they make efforts to improve their behavior. Ariel, for example, says, "[S]ome do it to make boys like them. I do it 'cuz it just me...this is how I'm *raised*, you know, my mom's loud" (p. 164). But Ariel now describes this behavior thus: "[I]t's like you trying to draw attention" (p. 168) and "[T]here's no sense, it's ignorant" (p. 168). And she says that Black girls "*are* being stereotyped each moment on whatever we do" (pp. 168–169). In the end, Ariel "did calm *down* so they give me more respect, they speak to me. I wouldn't really wanna talk or hang around anybody that's real loud. That's kinda embarrassing" (p. 168).

Even when disadvantaged Black female students do not "calm down," the evidence suggests that their aggression is mostly confined to other Black female students and they seem genuinely puzzled that their teachers are unable to help them. Pugh-Lilly, Neville, and Poulin (2001), for example, conducted extensive interviews with 11 Black female teenagers from poor or working-class families who were attending an alternative school after being expelled from their regular schools for fighting. The students in the study say they are constantly faced with situations where they feel they have to make a choice: either they "face down" the other student, that is, act aggressively, or they "hold off," that is, avoid conflict and report what happened to an adult. If they hold off, however, their parents will criticize them for not defending themselves (Marcella says her mother "was mad at me because I didn't fight the girl back," p. 149), and if they defend themselves they will be unfairly punished (when Tracy tried to justify her actions to her principal, the principal "still said that I'm put out and I said 'Why?' He said, 'I wasn't there. I don't know what really went on, so I'm gonna put everybody out,'" pp. 150–151).

Most disadvantaged Black female students are neither loud nor physically aggressive. The challenge they face is low teacher expectations. Thompson (2002) introduces us to Celeste, a high school senior hoping to attend college. We are told that "from the beginning, Celeste struggled with reading" and "even though she could not read, she was promoted to the next grade year after year. In her opinion, early on, teachers gave up on her" (p. 27). Celeste in turn almost gave up on her teachers: "In fifth grade, a teacher forced me to read and I felt bad. I was trying to read and kids were laughing at me. So I just got up and left. My house was right down the street, so I just got up and went home and just stayed there. I got in trouble by my mom. When I told her, she understood" (p. 23). It was not until the end of 10th grade that Celeste "finally got the help that she needed, when an RSP teacher began to teach her how to decode words" (p. 25): "Learning phonics made a big difference for me....I felt good when I didn't have to copy other people" (p. 25). At the time the study was published, Celeste was still struggling to catch up—"I still don't know how to write an essay yet" (p. 25)—and applying to go to a historically Black college nearby.

Three Case Studies

Case studies give us insights into how poverty, minority status, and gender place students at greater risk of disengagement, academic failure, and disruptive behavior. Three case studies have been especially influential among researchers and practitioners in determining how they approach the education of at-risk students. Anyon (1997) studied a K–8 school in a Newark, New Jersey, "ghetto" in the early 1990s. "Marcy Elementary" had 500 students at the time, 61% African American and 37% Hispanic. Of the 500 students, 497 were eligible for free lunch. A psychological assessment of a random sample of students found that they were "plagued by the problems that result from poverty: chaotic lives, neglect, abuse, histories of poor health and chronic health problems, emotional stress, anxiety, and anger" (p. 15), and their "desperate lives" made many of them "restless and confrontational" (p. 28). Marcy was staffed by 25 full-time teachers, including 16 Black and 6 Hispanic teachers. Most of the teachers were frustrated by their inability to control their students: "Perhaps fueled by this frustration, many of these black teachers were—to varying degrees—abusive of their students" (p. 28), and some teachers were observed hitting, shaking, and verbally abusing their students. Though one Black teacher said, "'It's what they're used to. They wouldn't listen to us if we didn't yell and put on a mean face. They know it's only our school voice'" (p. 29), Anyon says that what she observed "goes beyond any tradition of harsh discipline that would be generally sanctioned among other African Americans" (p. 30):

> The staff's abusive, implicitly sanctioned attitudes and behaviors have evolved over time in a situation where working conditions make teaching and administering extremely difficult and in a milieu in which the student population is extremely poor, racially marginalized, often of low academic standing and difficult to motivate educationally, and from families with little or no social clout. (p. 31)

Ogbu (2003), as we have already noted, studied Black students in Shaker Heights, Ohio, an upper-middle-class suburb of Cleveland with 58% White households and 32.6% Black households. Though Shaker Heights Black students' achievement test scores were higher than the scores of Black students elsewhere in the state and in the country as a whole, they were significantly lower than the scores of Shaker Heights White students. Ogbu describes Black students beginning elementary school believing they could perform as well as White students and as fully engaged with their school work. Long before they left high school, however, these students had come to believe that Black students generally and they themselves were not as capable as White students. By this phase of their school careers the students were doing just enough work to get by in lower-level classes, which required little homework, and focusing their energies on watching TV, talking with friends on the phone, playing sports, and working part-time jobs. Black students in Shaker Heights said that their teachers did not push them as hard as they pushed White students. When they rushed through their assignments or hurried to answer teachers' questions without understanding them, their White teachers called this "Black learning style" (p. 26). Ogbu found that

Black parents did not participate as much in their children's school-related activities as White parents. Their attendance at open houses is said to be "poor" and their participation in an academic support program is described as "dismal" (p. 222). For Ogbu the significant contrast is between immigrant (or voluntary) minorities, such as those from Asia or the Pacific Islands, who place pragmatic trust in the school system to reward them if they work hard and stay out of trouble, and the mistrust and alienation of nonimmigrant (or involuntary) minorities, such as African Americans or Native Indians, who oppose and resist schools as imposed by Whites to keep them inferior. Finally, Fordham (1996, 2001), as we have also noted, compared high-achieving and under-achieving female and male students at an overwhelmingly Black high school in Washington, DC, in the early 1980s. In a context where schooling was commonly perceived to be "White" and making an effort to succeed in school was seen to be "acting White," "resistance—both as conformity and avoidance—to the hegemony of whiteness was a primary finding of the study" (Fordham, 2001, p. 142). While high-achieving students resist "dominant claims of Black people's intellectual inadequacy by consciously conforming to school norms and expectations, underachieving students resist through avoidance" (Fordham, 1996, p. 283). All of the underachieving male students in the study had received above-average grades in elementary school but showed a steep downward trend from junior high school onward: "The major cause of the lessened effort and lower grades appears to have been the emerging sense of manhood, which was repeatedly negated by the 'master status'…of Blackness coupled with a desire for acceptance by the changing peer group" (p. 286). At home, the underachieving male students were taught to "preserve gender domination (for survival in the Black community)" (p. 148): "[A]s these young males reached puberty and entered high school, their mothers appear to have adopted a relationship style that closely approximates that which they have with adult males who are the objects of their love and affection" (p. 171) and, as we have already noted, they seek their sons' approval by not criticizing them and not setting limitations. At school, where "black teachers … are often perceived to be 'functionaries' of the dominant society" (Fordham, 2001, p. 145), "black students' reluctance to embrace the values reflected in school-sanctioned practices undermines their teachers' confidence in their ability to master the prescribed knowledge" (p. 146). For Black males especially it took extraordinary efforts to do their school work unaffected by parents who did not discipline them, by teachers who had little confidence in their ability, and by peers who might reject them. One student, who "lived in one of the federally subsidized housing projects that feed into Capital, a place where it is definitely a no-no for males to be caught with books of any kind" (Fordham, 1996, p. 94), put his books under his jacket before he left school. Another student, while still in elementary school, "had deliberately chosen for friends individuals who would act as protectors in exchange for his help on homework assignments and tests. He had not been picky about who they were" (p. 246). In explaining Black students' resistance to Whiteness, Fordham (2001) says, "Having been either totally excluded from publicly supported schooling both during enslavement and for approximately one hundred years thereafter, African American students who were born and schooled during the Second Emancipation [i.e., during desegregation] resist their recent inclusion—as internalization—in the American school system" (p. 156).

Critical Race Theory in Education

Severely disadvantaged ethnic minority students clearly face the most intractable barriers to school involvement. We have described poor Black and Hispanic students at Marcy Elementary in Newark, New Jersey, who are restless and confrontational and Black and Hispanic teachers who no longer seem able to separate discipline from abuse. But Marcy is a school that serves some of the most distressed families in one of New Jersey's most distressed cities, and it is not clear to the researcher, or her readers, whether anything short of re-building the community as a whole could be of much help. We have also described less disadvantaged Black students in Washington, DC, and middle-class Black students in Shaker Heights, Ohio, resisting efforts by their teachers to involve them in classroom activities. The issues here are more complex, involving both ethnicity and socioeconomic status, and these factors can work together or independently. Generally, however, many disadvantaged and ethnic minority students come to see urban schools as representing the interests of a larger middle-class White community which seeks to undermine their attachment to their local communities. Fine (1995) makes this view explicit with reference to class when she says that "public schools in low-income neighborhoods often represent themselves as the means for low-income students to 'escape' their local communities—sometimes a way to save 'those students' from 'those parents'" (p. 86). Fordham (1996) and Ogbu (2003) make the point with reference to ethnicity when they describe Black student resistance to perceived threats to their identity as African Americans, including the apparent desire of some Black students to escape that identity. Fordham (1996) reinforces the point by showing that when school involvement is not perceived to be a threat to their identity, students do not resist. For example, she describes a sort of grudging acceptance among their peers of some students (especially girls) who conform to their teachers' expectations in the belief that the knowledge they acquire will benefit their families in the future and she notes that an exception is routinely made for athletes (especially boys) who are striving for excellence in one of the few areas they can see where the larger White community allows Blacks to succeed on the basis of merit.

We know that in schools where students and teachers see themselves as members of the same community, working together toward a common goal, student discipline and academic achievement tend to be positive. It is no surprise that some of the most successful schools today are located in middle-class White suburbs and are staffed by middle-class White teachers. But it is also true that some of the nation's most successful schools in the past were located in poor, segregated African American communities and were staffed by poorly paid Black teachers. As one historian has said, "[T]hese schools became places notable for their exemplary teachers, their curriculum and extracurricular activities, their parental involvement, and the leadership of school principals" (Siddle Walker, 2003, p. 59). Though separate Black education continues today in independent Black schools, African-centered magnet schools in public school districts, and in de facto separate schools in predominantly African American communities, for every school that manages to overcome the remaining barrier between middle-class teachers and disadvantaged students there seems to be another school where socioeconomic barriers alone prove to be insurmountable. Since desegregation, however, the vast majority of disadvantaged Black students have attended schools staffed largely by middle-class White teachers. The challenge faced by these schools is to increase student involvement by building school communities which students and teachers from different class and ethnic backgrounds possess in common.

Recent research on school desegregation emphasizes the significance of continuing disparities in the education of White and African American children (Brown, Beckett, & Beckett, 2006). Researchers use the failure of school desegregation, especially in the north and west, to explain persisting gaps in White and Black school funding and teacher qualifications which place Black students at greater risk of educational failure. The overall failure of school desegregation is convincingly explained by critical race theory. In fact it is the Supreme Court's decision in *Brown v. Board of Education* [347 U.S. 483 (1954)] and its consequences that provide critical race theorists with their main bridge from the theory's origins in legal studies to its adopted home in education. According to Ladson-Billings and Tate (1995), "Today, students of color are more segregated than ever before" (p. 55), and this means that "race continues to be a factor in determining inequity in the United States" (p. 48). Ladson-Billings and Tate, like other critical race theorists, argue that U.S. society is based on property rights rather than human rights. They interpret the civil rights legislation of the 1950s and 1960s, for example, as having less to do with promoting equality at home than with defending the property interests of White Americans in increasingly hostile third world countries during the cold war. In applying critical race theory to education, Ladson-Billings and Tate argue that the U.S. legal system generally is designed to camouflage the property interests of Whites, and numerous researchers have pointed out that while the *Brown* decision speaks eloquently of equality, in interpreting the decision in the 1960s and 1970s federal judges severely limited its scope and application. Most important in the present context, Ladson-Billings and Tate argue that school desegregation legislation benefited Whites as much as it did Blacks. For critical race theorists, the *Brown* decision is an example of interest convergence. While it encouraged Blacks to fight for better urban schools, *Brown* also encouraged many Whites to flee to the suburbs, where they could provide a stronger tax base for their schools. *Brown* also convinced urban White communities of the necessity of seizing control of local school district resources to provide quality magnet, advanced placement, and gifted programs for their children, while assigning Black children to poorly funded general programs and to federally supported programs for students with special needs.

Critical race theory's notion of interest convergence helps us see how self-interest can motivate a dominant middle-class White community to absorb some of the apparent advances made by subordinate Black communities. In education, critical race theory seems necessary if we are to understand the *Brown* decision on school segregation and some of its consequences. In this book, however, we challenge critical race theorists to consider revising their original dominant/subordinate premise to eliminate its residual racism. We ask specifically whether we can now see in urban schools not just individuals and communities limited to pursuing their own interests regardless of the interests of others but also more and more individuals and communities coming together to build shared spaces where all children are promised the opportunity to succeed. Our intention is to show that given the opportunity to construct a new alternative school for at-risk students and being convinced that their own interests would be satisfied, Black and White and disadvantaged and middle-class students, teachers, parents, and administrators in one Midwestern school district found a way to work together to resolve the remaining issues which divided them and to create an alternative school they could possess in common.

Ladson-Billings (1999) says that critical race theory is an "important intellectual and social tool for deconstruction, reconstruction, and construction—deconstruction of oppressive structures and discourses, reconstruction of human agency, and construction of equitable and socially just relations of power" (p. 10). Critical race theory strives to achieve these aims in part by giving the victims of racial oppression the opportunity to "name their own reality," for by sharing their stories among themselves and with their oppressors Black students and teachers expose and help to undermine racism, heal the psychic wounds caused by oppression, and begin the process of building a new, equitable social reality. But critical race theory must also acknowledge that the deconstruction of oppressive structures and discourses requires the active participation of all victims of racism, that the reconstruction of human agency in predominantly African American school communities requires strong principal leadership as well as exemplary teachers, and that the construction of socially equitable and just relations of power is an on-going struggle that already has a long history. Though Black principals were criticized during segregation as beneficiaries of racism, recent scholarship has shown that most Black principals were strong school leaders best described as survivors of racism whose efforts were indispensable to the survival of their schools and communities. In this book we seek to extend this work by giving voice to one Black principal who led an alternative school community in the post-*Brown* era and who had to overcome lingering racism to convince district administrators that the school was viable, to show predominantly White teachers that their students were willing and able to learn, to motivate poor Black and Appalachian students to engage in school-related activities, and to encourage Black and White parents to become involved in their children's education.

Conclusion

We have seen that poverty and minority status are insufficient explanations for urban students' academic disengagement and disruptive behavior. For every child who is restless and confrontational as a result of problems associated with poverty at home, there are at least two children who, though clearly capable of success, are unwilling to cooperate. But responding effectively to the cultural needs of low-income and ethnic minority students can be even more daunting than trying to satisfy their physical and emotional needs, and the result is that teachers and administrators in regular schools may give up on at-risk students and transfer them to alternative schools. This places alternative schools at the center of economic, cultural, political, and historical forces which seem to guarantee their failure. Located in urban districts serving large numbers of low-income and ethnic minority families, enrolling students perceived by regular school teachers to be the worst of the worst, wrapped up in a social and political dynamic that discourages serious educational engagement, and trapped in a history that offers little hope for the future—alternative schools can seem only one step removed from an open admission of educational failure.

The problem with this analysis lies in its presentation of low-income ethnic minority students who are at risk of educational failure. The behavior of at-risk students may be the "worst" teachers face, and its persistence may justify them in thinking the students are the worst as well, but the evidence presented in this chapter indicates that traditional school environments are contributing factors and that the behavior of at-risk students is likely to improve in appropriate alternative school settings. Focusing on the experience of disadvantaged African American children and youth, we have seen that most female students are willing to engage with teachers and administrators on issues that separate them and are often successful in resolving them and that academic disengagement and problem behavior is not a major issue for Black male students until they reach 4th grade and the demands placed on them to achieve academically begin to increase. This evidence leads us to suggest that if Fordham (1996) is correct when she says that African American students in traditional schools resist "dominant claims of Black people's intellectual inadequacy" (p. 283) and that it is the academically weaker students who resist through avoidance, disengagement, and disruption, alternative schools which focus their efforts of providing quality remedial programs and which are staffed by teachers with a record of success teaching

African American students can tap into the stronger desire of Black students to resist through conformity and demonstrated competence.

Chapter 3

Students Placed at Risk: Classroom Routines, School Rules, and Alienated Youth

Introduction

IN MANY suburban schools today, students, teachers, and parents see themselves as members of a single learning community working toward a common goal. Why is this type of cooperation more difficult to achieve in so many of our urban schools? What prevents some students from participating more fully in their teachers' classroom activities, making it more likely that they will be restless and disruptive? What keeps some urban parents from becoming more involved in their children's school-related activities and makes it less likely that they will give them the support they need to succeed? If the challenge faced by urban schools is to increase student and parent involvement by building school communities which students, parents, and teachers possess in common, what exactly are the barriers that have to be overcome before they can succeed?

Classroom Routines

We have seen that low-income and ethnic minority students are more disruptive and are punished more often and more severely than other students. To understand this phenomenon better, researchers have focused on what they perceive to be pervasive cross-cultural miscommunication in urban classrooms with increasing numbers of low-income African American students and increasing numbers of middle-class White teachers (Cooper & Jordan, 2003). Cross-cultural miscommunication may find expression in the way teachers organize their classrooms. Hale-Benson (1989), for example, argues that White teachers use different criteria when grouping Black students than the students use when grouping themselves:

> Through ability grouping, children receive messages of relationship from the teacher. If the wrong children are assigned to the lower-ability group, they will reject the messages of relationship from the teacher....The social work between White teachers and Black children in the areas of status and identity is such a failure that the children turn off and physiologically shut down. (pp. 86–87)

Cross-cultural miscommunication also finds expression in the way teachers and students interact. Vavrus and Cole (2002), for example, studied what they call the "disciplinary moment," that is, the one disruptive act among many that is singled out by teachers for punishment. They found that "this singling-out process...disproportionately affects students whose race and gender distance them from their teachers" (p. 109), making it more difficult for teachers to interpret students' behavior correctly. Townsend (2000) also observes that "the combined effect of race and class differences often means that African American students' behaviors are likely to be misinterpreted by school personnel" and that "those misinterpretations contribute to the disconnection of African American students from school settings" (p. 385). Pervasive cross-cultural miscommunication can create what Scott, Nelson, and Liaupsin (2001) call "aversive situations," that is, classrooms characterized by student–teacher conflict. In aversive situations Black students intentionally engage in disruptive behavior and White teachers routinely respond by having the students removed from the classroom. These situations are common in urban classrooms because "removal from instruction constitutes negative reinforcement for *both* student and teacher, in that their behaviors (classroom disruption, removing the student from the classroom, respectively) lead to termination of an aversive situation" (p. 314).

Researchers who have studied cross-cultural miscommunication in urban classrooms describe a common situation in which Black students interrupt and speak out loudly and White teachers, interpreting the behavior as disrespectful, respond by taking disciplinary action. The problem is that the students' intention is often to show interest and to participate, and when their teachers react negatively they feel confused, hurt, and angry. In explaining how this situation arises, researchers contrast Black culture, which they describe as highly dynamic and as emphasizing multi-tasking and group activities, and our historically White public school culture, which is more restrained and in which students are expected to work individually on one task at a time. When Black students interrupt and speak out loudly they are trying to make a contribution to what they perceive to be a group activity, but White teachers, seeing the activity as an opportunity to engage with students one at a time on their individual learning projects, tend to view the behavior as a challenge to their authority and react accordingly. The tragedy in many urban classrooms is that over time students come to see their behavior in the same way their teachers do, and some students decide to continue interrupting and speaking out loudly, the only difference being that they now do it in a deliberate attempt to be disrespectful.

The issue raised by research on cross-cultural miscommunication is whether the disproportionate punishment of low-income and ethnic minority students is a result of teacher bias or of higher rates of student misbehavior. Researchers who have tried to disentangle these factors report that while both are clearly involved, teacher bias may be the more significant factor. Skiba (2001), a leading researcher in this area, contrasts the higher rate of punishment of boys, which "may often be an accurate response to the tendency of boys to engage in a higher rate of misbehavior" (p. 181), with the higher rate of punishment of African American students, who are "disciplined more frequently and harshly for more subjective and less serious reasons" (p. 182). Among the individual studies that tend to support this view, Hughes, Gleason, and Zhang (2005) found that 1st grade teachers in Texas report having poorer relationships with African American students than with White or Hispanic students, even after controlling for educational level. Downey and Pribesh (2004) found that while teachers generally rate Black students as poorer classroom citizens than White students, Black students placed with same-race teachers are rated more favorably than White students. After reviewing research on the disproportionate punishment of ethnic minority students, and reporting her own findings on the punishment of African American boys, Arnett Ferguson (2000) concludes that

> a systematic racial bias is exercised in the regulation, control, and discipline of children in the United States today. African American males are apprehended and punished for misbehavior and delinquent acts that are overlooked in other children. The punishment that is meted out is usually more severe than for other children. This racism that systematically extinguishes the potential and constrains the world of possibilities for black males would be brutal enough if it were restricted to school, but it is replicated in other disciplinary systems of the society, the most obvious parallel being the juvenile justice system. (pp. 233–234)

One challenge faced by middle-class White teachers today is to overcome a racial bias that may lead them to misinterpret Black students' behavior and to punish them unfairly. A second challenge, one which was faced by middle-class African American teachers in Black schools during and after segregation, is to overcome a class bias that may lead them to underestimate the potential of low-income Black students and to further alienate them from classroom activities. Rist (1973/2002) and Gouldner (1978) conducted separate multi-year ethnographic studies in K–2 classrooms in all-Black schools in the 1960s and 1970s. Gouldner (1978) found that teachers "encouraged the evolution of three groups of students who were taught differently and often separately" (p. 129): a "high" group, most of whom were girls, received "a disproportionate amount of teaching time and positive response" (p. 130); "middle" and "low" ability groups "toed the line … compliantly and did not interfere with the learning of the top group" (p. 130); and a separate group of "troublesome boys" "received a lot of attention of a negative sort" (p. 130). Rist (1973/2002) observed that kindergarten students were permanently assigned on the eighth day of school to one of three tables, and that "[t]he single most influential variable to which the teachers responded was the social class background of the student" (p. 242). The effects of the teachers' differential treatment of students are perhaps best seen in the behavior of the students themselves. Rist (1973/2002) says that

> one of the seemingly inescapable consequences of the segregation systems was that the children themselves quickly picked up what it meant to be on one side of the barrier or the other. Each group of students began to emulate the teacher's treatment of the other. The high group followed the teacher in their ridicule, belittlement, physical abuse, and social ostracism of the lower groups….The lower-class students displayed patterns of deference and passivity towards those of the high group. (p. 245)

All-Black schools in the 1960s and 1970s were continuing a tradition of separate Black education in which the primary role of schools and colleges was to strengthen Black communities by providing a sound academic training to future community leaders. By the 1980s and 1990s, however, this emphasis was changing, and more attention was being paid to strengthening Black communities by providing opportunities for academic, social, and personal development to all Black children. When Foster (1990, 1993, 1997) decided to base a study of African American pedagogy on interviews with 18 exemplary Black teachers working in integrated school systems, her intention was to test the common assumption at the time that Black teachers were "uncaring, unsympathetic, rigid individuals who, regardless of their class origins, neither identify with nor relate well to their working-class African-American pupils" (1990, p. 123). Though she hesitated to describe these exemplary teachers as "overly affectionate," Foster (1993) concluded that as a group they were "concerned individuals who commanded respect, were respectful of pupils, and who, although caring were strict in requiring all students to meet high academic and behavioral standards" (p. 377). Knowing that White teachers didn't expect Black students to succeed and that the students would be further discriminated against as adults, a Black teacher had to be an "admonisher, urger, and meddler." As one teacher put it, "The kids say, 'Well, I've got a C, so hey, that's wonderful.' But, see nobody Black would let him get away with that" (Foster, 1990, p. 134). Foster (1993) also noted that half of the teachers she interviewed used parental terms and family metaphors to describe their relationships with students and that in their discussions of personal influences on their teaching the most common references were to church events and pageants where "everyone had a part—even if it was as a lamb" (p. 384). This led Foster (1993) to conclude that the teachers saw themselves as surrogate parents and perceived classroom teaching and learning to be a family activity: regardless of the students' social class background, they were all part of the same classroom family and each one had a valuable contribution to make.

Howard (2001, 2002) further explored an aspect of African American pedagogy that has come to be called "culturally relevant teaching." He describes teachers who feel a connection with their students' families and communities (they often ask about students' families, lead discussions of community events in morning circle, and place a strong emphasis on rituals and routines to build community in their classrooms), whose modes of interaction remind students of their parents (stern and strict; passionate in praise and criticism; respectful in address—"Mister" and "Miss"—in providing explanations, and in setting high standards, and whose students respond positively because they believe their teachers care about them (one class makes an extra effort to be good after their teacher breaks down in tears while talking about the recent death of her father). Stanford (1998) explored a second aspect of African American pedagogy often referred to as "othermothering," basing her study on an analysis of what 11 award-winning Black teachers wrote about their own most memorable teacher. These "remembered teachers" are described as othermothers who were caring, nurturing, and always available and who emphasized "lifting as we climb," that is, racial uplift and "giving forward," or teaching students who would strengthen the community in the future. Stanford says that for poor students of color, "supportive relationships with teachers enable them to succeed in spite of adverse circumstances in their homes and communities" (p. 241). "Cheryl," one of the teachers in the study, grew up poor and attended segregated Black schools in Chicago in the 1940s. Her mother was chronically ill and often unable to comb Cheryl's hair or dress her for school. She remembers her 2nd grade teacher taking the time to comb her hair and leaving a pair of gloves or a hat in her desk. Fifty years later, teaching in a similar school in Chicago, Cheryl keeps a comb, brush, washcloths, and soap for her own students to use.

Studies of culturally responsive classrooms also show how African American teachers defuse potentially aversive situations without resorting to removing students from instruction. Monroe and Obidah (2004), for example, describe a Black teacher who responded to inappropriate but not intentionally disruptive behavior by humorously acknowledging stereotypes of her low-income African American students' abilities and immediately re-directing their attention to academic work they were clearly expected to master. When faced with deliberately disruptive behavior, however, this teacher responded with demonstrations of emotion and affect, delivered in a firm, authoritative manner that mirrored "the blunt and direct types of discipline to which many urban African American students from low-income backgrounds are exposed in their homes" (p. 265). Case (1997), to take a second example, introduces us to Alma, an experienced elementary teacher in an inner-city school in the northeast: "When I first had this class, their faces were hanging down to the floor, their attitudes were off the wall. I had never seen such unhappy children....I just couldn't believe the first couple of days. They were at each other's throats" (pp. 34–35). Alma succeeds in creating a strong community of learners in her classroom by focusing on learning discipline first and by re-directing their unhappiness outward toward people who look down on them:

> You have to have them experience some success, and you set your guidelines. Those classroom rules were taught as if they were a lesson the first two weeks of school. We role-played them. I do them once a month now, and when they open up in the morning, after they've said their pledge, they say, "In Room 376, we always strive

to be number one." They say it every day, and they feel like they're number one and work like they're number one. (p. 35)

She also tells them that "daily, you will face someone who feels that the color of your skin is more important than who you are. So, just look them in the eye, and say I deserve to be here" (p. 35).

Tyson (2003) makes explicit one important theme that emerges from recent studies of African American pedagogy. She says that her findings in 3rd and 4th grade classrooms in two all-Black schools "support Fordham's (1996) claim that black teachers regularly practice resistance by trying to ensure that their students do not fit negative stereotypes....These teachers' resistance is to the dominant representation and stereotypes of blacks and black culture, and it is practiced as conformity to mainstream norms—hence the tendency to hold students to the highest and strictest standards of behavior" (p. 339). But the question to be raised here is what is there to motivate most public school teachers today if the majority of teacher education students in the 1990s were, as Stanford (1998) notes, "White, female, monolingual, and from a rural, small-town, or suburban community with limited experiences with individuals from other cultures" (p. 241)? And what is there to motivate our future teachers if teacher education programs today mostly enroll White pre-service teachers who are less willing than their African American counterparts to teach Black students (Bakari, 2003)? Can we envisage future classrooms in which teachers are prepared to resist any representation or stereotype that might limit their students' futures?

Murtadhu-Watts (2000) makes explicit a second theme that emerges from studies of African American pedagogy. On the basis of his study of a K–7 school in Detroit designed to provide African American–centered education by Black male teachers for Black male students, he agrees with Black educators who "recognize that students should learn to read and write in meaningful contexts" but who "also defend the perspective that the teaching of skills in a quiet, controlled environment is absolutely essential to black students' survival" (p. 66). What is there in the training of most public school teachers to meet the needs of disadvantaged Black students to master basic skills in a quiet, controlled classroom environment when teacher education programs place more emphasis on learning to read and write in meaningful contexts? Can we envisage future classrooms in which teachers are adequately trained in the full range of pedagogical options and equipped to make pedagogical choices based on the needs of their students?

School Rules

Cross-cultural miscommunication in urban classrooms helps explain why teachers disproportionately refer low-income and ethnic minority students to the office for disciplinary action. But the widespread belief among low-income and ethnic minority parents that their children are punished unfairly is also connected to their perception that urban schools' disciplinary policies are culturally biased. Researchers have traced the roots of this perception of unfairness to different standards of childrearing arising in different socioeconomic and ethnic cultures. Lareau (1996), for example, found that middle-class White parents in a small Midwestern city supported teachers when they told students not to "hit back," whereas working-class minority parents in a large northeastern city were more likely to encourage their children to "defend" themselves. Furthermore, Cook and Fine (1995) found that middle-class White parents living in areas with low levels of crime and violence allowed their children more personal freedom, confident they would develop self-discipline, whereas low-income African American parents living in areas with high levels of crime and violence were more directive and controlling of their children, fearing they would not always be able to protect them. Given these different standards of childrearing, many working-class parents believe that school policies that dictate zero tolerance for fighting, for instance, unfairly punish their children for trying to protect themselves, and many African American parents believe that school policies that ignore minor transgressions, treating them as opportunities to develop self-discipline, are unfair because they encourage behaviors that place their children at greater risk of more serious transgressions.

Many urban schools have been successful in developing new discipline policies and programs that reduce overall student referrals and suspensions and expulsions for all categories of misbehavior (Brown & Beckett, 2006). These interventions are complex and varied, reflecting the different concerns they are intended to address and the different stakeholders involved in their development. Generally, however, school disciplinary policies and programs can be categorized as following either an instructional or a legal approach to misbehavior, depending on whether they seek to improve student behavior or to respond effectively to student misbehavior. The question to be raised here is whether there is cultural bias in the development and implementation of either or both types of policy. Do the instructional and legal approaches to discipline address the concerns of low-income parents that schools punish their children unfairly when they try to defend themselves? Do they address the concerns of African American parents that schools encourage their children to behave in ways that place them at increased risk of committing serious infractions? We raise these questions because, regardless of the progress that has been made in many schools, it remains as true today as it was in the past that low-income and ethnic minority students are punished more often and more severely than other students and their parents still believe their children are being punished unfairly.

The instructional approach to student discipline, which is described by proponents as positive, proactive, and preventive, has been gaining in popularity for at least the past 25 years. Research by the Phi Delta Kappa Commission on Discipline in the early 1980s indicated that in schools with good discipline the emphasis was on positive behaviors and preventive measures, with punishment being used only as a last resort. According to the commission, "exemplary schools do not concentrate their efforts on formal rule enforcement or punishment programs. Instead, they engage in a wide range of activities designed to enhance the self-perceptions of students and to maintain the support and confidence of staff members" (Lasley & Wayson, 1982, p. 30). Perhaps the most widely used instructional approach to discipline today is positive behavior support, a comprehensive program including primary interventions, which teach and reinforce pro-social behaviors in all students; secondary interventions, which involve specialized programs for groups of students seen to be at risk for problem behavior; and tertiary interventions, which are specialized supports for individual students who exhibit chronic and intense problem behavior (George, Harrower, & Knoster, 2003). But is the instructional approach's emphasis on enhancing the self-perceptions and pro-social behaviors of students culturally biased? From what we have learned of Black students' oppositional behavior and of low-income students' belief in the importance of standing up for themselves, it is not clear that their self-perceptions need to be enhanced or that their behavior is necessarily anti-social. Furthermore, is the approach's emphasis on instruction itself culturally biased, implying, as the Phi Delta Kappa commission found, a de-emphasizing of the strict application of school rules? Working within the instructional approach, would not teachers and administrators seek every opportunity to encourage students to learn from their experiences and to develop self-discipline, and unintentionally place African American students at greater risk for more serious forms of misbehavior?

The instructional approach was conceived and developed in opposition to traditional legal approaches to student discipline, which by the 1980s had come to be seen as negative, reactive, and punitive. This opposition is still evident today. According to one of its leading proponents, the instructional approach is based on the assumption that "finding ways to produce safe and orderly schools need not compel us to turn schools into prisons or detention centers. It should be possible to create more schools...where high academic achievement is the norm, and discipline problems are the exception" (Noguera, 2003, p. 350). Support for this assumption can be found in the results of several recent studies which compare demographically matched schools with high and low suspension rates. In Chapter 2, we cited the example of a Florida school district where it was found that in schools with high out-of-school suspension rates, the focus was on punishment of inappropriate behavior, whereas schools with low out-of-school suspension rates focused on social skills training for students and behavioral management training for teachers (Raffaele Mendez, Knoff, & Ferron, 2002). When a similar study was conducted in Kentucky, researchers found that in schools with low student suspension rates the emphasis was on the importance of keeping students involved and connected through extra-curricular activities (Christle, Nelson, & Jolivette, 2004). Teachers at a middle school which had one of the lowest suspension rates in the state said that only a "couple" of their students were not involved in at least one of the school's many clubs and sports teams.

The problem with these studies and with the instructional approach generally is related to cause and effect. No one doubts that a well-designed instructional program properly implemented will have a positive effect on school climate generally and on the behavior of at least some students. But the issue is whether this can be accomplished in schools which are not already safe and orderly, and in which students are not already prepared to learn. From the Florida study it is not clear whether schools reduced out-of-school suspensions because they implemented an instructional approach to discipline or whether schools which already had low student suspension rates decided to adopt instructional programs. Nor is it clear whether Kentucky schools had lower suspension rates because they involved students in extra-curricular activities or whether schools which already had lower suspension rates made greater efforts to keep students involved through extra-curricular activities. We raise the issue because in both of these studies, as well as in other studies we have cited, it was also found that schools with higher numbers of low-income and ethnic minority students had higher rates of suspension. It is not clear, then, whether and to what extent low-income and African American students in Florida and Kentucky responded positively to the instructional programs their schools adopted.

Even the most ardent proponents of the instructional approach to discipline recognize its limitations. Regardless of how successful a particular program may be, at least some students will not respond completely or consistently to more positive, proactive, and preventive approaches. In the second category of interventions designed to improve student discipline are policies and programs that follow a legal approach. After summarizing a range of research findings, a leading scholar in this area concluded that "schools whose rules for behavior are clear and firmly enforced; whose adults watch for misbehavior, recognize it when it occurs, and immediately punish it; and whose adults model desired behaviors and reward them when they occur experience less problem behavior" (Gottfredson, 2001, p. 84), and in reporting the results of one of her own studies, this scholar says that lower rates of teacher and student victimization correlate strongly with clarity and predictability regarding behavioral norms and consistency and fairness in the application of consequences (Gottfredson, 1997). Conversely, numerous studies have shown that in schools with high levels of problem behavior, rules for behavior are unclear, unfair, or inconsistently enforced; teachers and administrators either do not know the rules or disagree on them; and students do not believe in the legitimacy of the rules. These research findings would appear to be unambiguous, having been tested and re-tested over a period of decades. They would also seem to pass the test concerning possible cultural bias, simply reiterating what many low-income and African American parents have been saying for years—namely, that school rules should be clear, fair, and strictly enforced.

The issue of the clarity and fairness of school rules has been brought into sharp focus in the past ten years with the widespread adoption of zero-tolerance policies for serious student misbehavior (Brown & Beckett, 2006). Even though they are intended to leave school officials with little latitude or discretion in administering punishments, zero-tolerance policies have been criticized for resulting in the suspension of some students for relatively minor transgressions and in the disproportionately severe punishment of low-income, African American, and emotionally and behaviorally disordered students. District-wide studies have shown that the adoption of zero-tolerance policies has exacerbated long-standing discrepancies in the use of suspension and expulsion across schools. Though higher suspension rates, for example, correlate with higher levels of negative attitudes and problem behaviors among students, these district-wide studies also show that student race and teacher attitudes toward students make greater contributions to predicting suspension. The issue here is not zero tolerance itself, but what behaviors schools should not tolerate. All parents, perhaps especially low-income and ethnic minority parents, can agree that the possession of weapons and the possession and distribution of alcohol and prohibited drugs should not be tolerated. Parents can clearly see the effects of weapons, alcohol, and drugs in their communities, and they want to protect their children from them. But fighting is another issue. All parents can agree that bullying and other forms of physical and psychological intimidation should be dealt with severely, and low-income and African American parents know how, in the absence of effective law enforcement, "might is right" can quickly take hold in their communities. But the issue for many low-income and ethnic minority parents is that the victims of bullying, in the absence of effective rule enforcement in schools, can be punished for trying to defend themselves, and under zero-tolerance policies they can be punished as severely as the bullies themselves.

To begin to address the issues raised by cross-cultural miscommunication in urban classrooms, we looked to the parallel literature on culturally relevant teaching for insights. We found that Black teachers were strict but caring; they hold high expectations for their students' academic, social, and personal development but also were aware of the problems they bring with them from home. Here, to address the issues relating to the disproportionate punishment of low-income and African American students, we can look to a smaller body of literature on what might be called culturally relevant discipline. The question we ask is, How do African American principals in urban schools overcome cross-cultural miscommunication between their schools and low-income and African American families on the issue of student discipline? How do they respond to parents who believe that schools punish their children unfairly and who give this as a reason for not being more involved in their children's school-related activities? As we will see in the case studies reported below, Black principals are also strict but caring, holding high expectations for students' behavior but also aware that many students act out in school largely because of problems they cannot deal with at home. The difference is that as principals they are often in a better position than teachers to help individual students and their parents deal with these problems in ways that do not disrupt classroom instruction.

Bryant (1998) studied the implementation of a long-term school reform program at an inner-city K–5 school in the southeast. The program was unsuccessful in involving parents and community members under one African American principal in 1989–1990 but successful under a second Black principal in 1994–1995. Whereas the first principal was perceived by parents to be an "outsider," the second principal had the "ability to correctly 'read' the surrounding community and his relationship to it" (p. 47). For parents, the role of the school was to assist them in raising their children in difficult circumstances. The first principal seemed to deny this responsibility when a parent asked him to post an adult on a street corner near the school to stop older children fighting and allow younger children to pass safely. The first principal responded by saying that "children have to be taught alternatives to fighting at home" (p. 42). The second principal agreed with parents that the school was there to support them. In response to the belief of some parents that their children were being punished unfairly, he instituted a program under which the school social worker was asked "to shed light on behavioral problems that occur in the classroom and make recommendations to teachers based on detailed information of the children's home lives" (p. 46). The second principal then ensured that the social worker's findings were taken into account before a decision was made on whether to take "disciplinary or remedial action" (p. 46).

Case (1997), to take a second example, introduces us to Marguerite, a young principal at an elementary school in Connecticut. Marguerite would appear to take a legal approach to student discipline because she "sets firm expectations for the children" (p. 31), but her firm expectations are based on the belief that students feel empowered when they "know what the boundaries are" (p. 31). For Marguerite, "the whole business of empowerment is to be responsive to them and give them survival skills, because they still have to go home" (p. 31):

> This sixth grader I have has a Dad who sells drugs and a mom who's a prostitute, and he has to go home and deal with that every night. So when he has a bad day, I bring him to the office and I talk to him about what he could have done in this given situation and what he did do in the given situation, and I try to get him to recognize that the teacher doesn't deserve, nor do his classmates deserve, that kind of behavior. (p. 31)

Finally, Reitzug and Patterson (1998) describe Mrs. Presley, an African American middle school principal who adopted "a form of caring that empowered students by assisting them in identifying alternative ways of proceeding as they addressed the situations that confronted them" (p. 165). When a student gives her a letter describing the trouble he is having with one teacher, Mrs. Presley first exclaims, "[T]hat's a wonderful letter, Jesse! You have excellent writing ability. You express yourself very well. Yes, you have a gift! That's a real gift!" (p. 162). She then goes on to say:

> You know teachers, Jesse—they're all different. You have to learn how each of them teaches. Some teachers don't like to be interrupted when they're teaching. With those teachers you have to wait until they've all finished before you ask questions. Other teachers you can talk to. (p. 162)

Conclusion

Cross-cultural miscommunication in urban classrooms between increasing numbers of low-income and ethnic minority students and middle-class White teachers can lead to aversive situations that are commonly resolved by having students removed from the classroom and sent to the principal's office for disciplinary action. The challenge faced by many teachers in urban schools is to overcome the class and racial bias that separates them from their students and makes it more difficult for them to respond effectively to student behavior that has its roots in home environments which they may not be familiar with and which may necessitate new pedagogical and disciplinary approaches. In contrast, case studies of successful African American teachers show them to be strict but caring, setting high standards for academic achievement and appropriate behavior but also concerned to create in their classrooms something that many of their students do not have at home, namely, family-like environments in which all children feel they belong and are cared for.

Cross-cultural conflict is exacerbated by the fact that many low-income and ethnic minority parents believe that schools punish their children unfairly. The challenge faced by urban principals is to overcome cultural bias in their schools' disciplinary practices to ensure that over-tolerance for minor transgressions does not encourage some children to commit more serious infractions and that zero tolerance for major transgressions such as fighting does not conflict with what other students are learning at home. Successful African American principals, like successful African American teachers, are strict but caring. They are strict in the application of all school rules because students know what they are doing is wrong and because, given the neglect many suffer at home, to show leniency would be to send the message that they do not care. But the strict application of school rules also helps create a safe, secure, and predictable environment in which students can feel empowered, something which their home lives may deny them, and it gives principals more opportunities to work one on one with students to help them understand behaviors such as fighting and to give them choices for the future.

Chapter 4

Parent Involvement: Support or Partnership?

Introduction

PARENTS' INVOLVEMENT in their children's school-related activities is associated with improved student behavior and academic achievement (Brown & Beckett, in press). Parent involvement promotes social control, that is, a consistent set of rules regarding appropriate behavior that can be communicated to students at home and at school. Parent involvement also increases parents' social capital, that is, their school-related skills and information, enabling them to give students more assistance in their academic work. But involving parents in their children's school-related activities is a challenge for large urban school districts with increasing numbers of disadvantaged minority parents and increasing numbers of middle-class White teachers. While most teachers believe that disadvantaged parents should be more involved in their children's schooling, many working-class and low-income parents feel that education is the responsibility of teachers, and while all teachers believe that parents should be involved in their children's schooling in positive ways, many African American parents are critical of school policies and programs they believe disadvantage their children.

Barriers to communication across ethnic and socioeconomic lines in urban schools are being erected in an atmosphere of mutual defensiveness and distrust between White middle-class teachers and disadvantaged African American parents. Many Black parents believe that teachers blame them for their children's discipline problems and poor academic performance and that their children's failure in school reflects badly on them, as African Americans. At the same time, White teachers fear that Black parents hold them responsible for their children's failure and that their inability to discipline and motivate disadvantaged Black students may reflect a deep-seated and unconscious racism. Furthermore, research has shown that urban schools could do more to create opportunities for extended, meaningful, and positive communications between parents and teachers. The only opportunities generally available now are short parent–teacher conferences and special meetings set up when a child is having academic or disciplinary problems, in which teachers and parents have little difficulty maintaining existing barriers to meaningful communication.

In Chapter 3 we said that in schools where teachers and students see themselves as members of the same community working toward a common goal, student discipline and academic achievement tend to be positive. In this chapter we extend the argument and show that student discipline and academic achievement are also positive in schools where teachers and parents see themselves as belonging to the same community. We cite as examples predominantly White urban schools in which middle-class teachers serve middle-class families and predominantly Black schools in which middle-class teachers have overcome class bias to serve low-income and working-class families. In most urban schools today, however, cultural differences regarding the roles of teachers and parents in the area of student discipline still have to be overcome before a true sense of community can emerge. Gottfredson (2001) is clearly correct when she says that "cultural differences among administrators, teachers, parents, and students make it more difficult to develop shared norms about behavior" and that "delinquent peer cultures are more likely to flourish in the absence of shared norms for behavior" (p. 242).

Agreeing the Facts

The most recent evidence shows that fewer parents with high school education or less and fewer parents living below the poverty line attend school meetings, events, and student conferences, act as volunteers, serve on school committees, and participate in school fundraising than parents with a college education and parents living above the poverty line (Vaden-Kiernan & McManus, 2005). For Black non-Hispanic parents, on the other hand, the situation is mixed: though they attend school events, act as volunteers, and participate in fundraising at lower levels than White non-Hispanic parents, they attend school meetings at the same levels and student conferences at slightly higher levels than White non-Hispanic parents. This pattern of parent involvement has been roughly constant over the past 30 years. Moles (1993) reviewed large-scale surveys conducted in the 1970s and 1980s showing that levels of parental involvement depended on education and socioeconomic status but not on minority status. Though parents with less than high school education had less than half the levels of school contact of parents who had college degrees, and though parents with very low incomes were three times more likely to have low levels of contact with schools than high-income parents, "no differences were observed between white, black, and Hispanic parents in level of involvement, suggesting that factors associated with poverty and limited education exert more influence in school contacts than minority status" (p. 27). At the same time, a recent large-scale study in Texas found that 1st grade teachers reported having better relationships with White and Hispanic parents than with African American parents, and the researchers found that the lower relationship quality with Black parents affected teachers' perceptions of students' academic ability after controlling for student educational level (Hughes, Gleason, & Zhang, 2005).

These patterns of parent involvement have also been shown to exist at the school district level. Hess and Leal (2001), using data from the 1990 U.S. census organized by school district and a Council of Urban Boards of Education survey, looked at correlations between school district median income and percentage African American student enrollment and opportunities districts provided for parents to have input into issues such as budgeting, curriculum review, principal selection, and school closure. As expected, opportunities for involvement were greater in districts with higher median incomes. Interestingly, however, opportunities for involvement were also greater in districts with higher percentages of African American student enrollment. The researchers concluded that "the positive effect of the positive African American student enrollment variable suggests that decades of activism may have helped institutionalize a relatively high level of access" (pp. 483–484). At the same time, as the use of the term "activism" would suggest, parent involvement at the district level does not necessarily imply that African American parents are always involved in what school district officials might think are "positive" ways. As the researchers go on to say, "African Americans have long encountered discrimination in schools and been forced to resort to grassroots mobilization, electoral activities, and legal action to improve access to and the quality of education" (p. 484).

Clarifying the Issues

The challenges faced by urban schools trying to improve communication between middle-class White teachers and disadvantaged and ethnic minority parents have proved so intractable and are of such long standing that researchers in the area have begun to call for fundamental changes in parent–teacher relationships. Smrekar and Cohen-Vogel (2001), for example, argue that the role of parents as "supporters, helpers, and fund raisers" is no longer tenable and that it should be replaced by a role in which parents are seen as "decision makers, partners, and collaborators" (p. 87). Current research and practice in the area of parent involvement, however, is dominated by what can be called the "support" model. According to this model, the role of parents is to support the work of teachers at home and at school. We have seen that quantitative research conducted over the past 30 years has consistently shown that levels of parent involvement depend on socioeconomic status. During the same period, as we will see in the following section, qualitative studies have convincingly demonstrated that gaps in parent support reflect profound differences in the roles education plays in the lives of many working-class and middle-class families, and these differences affect the level of support working-class parents are prepared to give. Furthermore, while quantitative research over the past 30 years has shown that levels of parent involvement do not depend on minority status, we will see in a later section that qualitative studies have demonstrated that increased levels of minority, especially African American, parent involvement have been viewed by many teachers as undermining rather than supporting the work they are trying to do in schools. We argue that the challenges faced by urban schools trying to improve communication between teachers and parents can be traced to fundamental disagreements regarding the role parents should play in their children's education. We argue that if schools are to gain the benefits associated with increased positive parent involvement, teachers and parents must come together as true partners in an effort to overcome the issues that separate them.

Parent Involvement and Socioeconomic Class

In seeking explanations for the gaps between socioeconomic groups in levels of parent involvement in education, qualitative researchers emphasize two main themes that emerge from interviews with parents. First, low-income parents often say they want, but are unable, to be more involved in their children's schooling. In addition to facing restricted opportunities for interaction with teachers owing to work, child-care responsibilities, transportation, and so on, low-income parents also describe psychological and cultural barriers they face when communicating with teachers and school officials (Moles, 1993). These barriers include differences in educational level and socioeconomic status and also dialect or language differences, fear and distrust of schools as a result of their own experiences, feeling threatened by the authority of teachers (who have responsibility for a whole class), anxiety and defensiveness resulting from being contacted by schools only when their children get into trouble, and what disadvantaged parents perceive to be teachers' and school officials' racism, paternalism, and lower expectations for their children. But many low-income parents also indicate during interviews that they resist teachers' and school officials' efforts to get them more involved in their children's education because they believe such involvement is inappropriate and that they say they want to be more involved only because that is what teachers and schools officials want to hear.

Crozier (2000) and Cullingford and Morrison (1999) have shown that different levels of parent involvement in England reflect different roles schools play in the lives of many working-class and middle-class families. Crozier based his study on extensive interviews with parents and teachers at two secondary schools, one serving predominantly working-class families and the other serving predominantly middle-class families. He concludes his study by saying that whereas middle-class parents are regarded as "more visible and overtly interventionist" and "working-class parents appear to be passive in educational matters, only making themselves visible at parents' evenings," with the behavior of working-class parents being "interpreted by teachers as indifference and lack of support" (p. 47), the evidence shows that working-class parents are "supportive and watchful of their children's progress" (p. 48) but also that they are "reliant upon teachers' judgments and place their trust in them" (pp. 47–48). Cullingford and Morrison found that this perspective persists even in urban schools which receive additional funding to hire staff to coordinate parent involvement programs. In these schools, though "parents are seen to become more supportive of what goes on in school because they understand it" and "begin to reinforce some of the techniques and approaches at home so that there is no clash of personal or social styles" (p. 257), the fact remains that only 1% of parents help out at school, and most of these parents already have the social capital they need to assist their children in their academic work, but the vast majority of parents say they feel like outsiders and are assumed by school staff to lack the confidence and self-esteem required to participate in school activities.

In the United States, Lareau (1987, 2000) has come to similar conclusions on the basis in part of case studies of two elementary schools in the San Francisco Bay area in the 1980s. In these studies, she found that working-class parents attended parent–teacher conferences and school open houses and volunteered less often than professional middle-class parents. But the significance of Lareau's studies lies in the detailed portraits they allow her to paint of the different roles schools play in the lives of many working-class and middle-class families. For working-class parents at "Colton," school was like work: it was something to leave behind at the end of the day. Life, in contrast, involved evening and weekend socializing, mainly with relatives living nearby. School was also something parents expected their children to leave behind after graduation. Though Colton mothers "insisted" on high school graduation, they expressed only a "tentative interest in having their children attend college" (2000, p. 100). For "Prescott" parents, on the other hand, school was an important part of family life. Not only were they more involved at school during the day, but they monitored and reinforced their children's school work and read more often with them at home and socialized more often with other Prescott parents. Furthermore, "Prescott parents insisted that their children acquire college degrees, and many were tentatively in favor of post-graduate work" (2000, p. 102). Given the different roles education played in the lives of Prescott and Colton families, it was only to be expected that interactions between Prescott parents and teachers were "more frequent, more centered around academic matters, and much less formal" (1987, p. 78) than interactions between Colton parents and teachers.

Weininger and Lareau (2003) followed up on these early studies by looking more closely at the forms of interactions teachers have with middle-class and working-class parents. The researchers tape-recorded parent–teacher conferences in two elementary schools: working-class, ethnically diverse "Lower Richmond" and White middle-class "Swan." The working-class parents at Lower Richmond appeared uncomfortable and did not talk much during the conferences. They are characterized as having been overly dependent on the teachers for student evaluations, for example, not persisting in criticisms they had of disciplinary actions taken against their children when their criticisms were rebuffed by the teachers. During most of the time allotted for the conferences at Lower Richmond, teachers are said to have "lectured" the parents. The middle-class parents at Swan, on the other hand, appeared comfortable in their conferences and talked a lot. In fact, they often "took over" the conferences, directing the conversation to areas of concern, volunteering information, asking specific, almost exclusively academic questions, probing for areas of weakness their children might have where their help might be needed, offering their own assessments of their children's abilities, and assuming an authority to persist in advocacy of their children or criticism of the teacher. Swan parents are generally described as having a strong "feel for the game" of parent–teacher conferences and an ability to use them for their own purposes.

Recent studies of urban schools in the United States serving predominantly low-income and working-class families also emphasize the fact that, just as parents resist greater involvement in their children's schools, teachers resist greater involvement in what they consider to be family concerns. O'Connor (2001) interviewed parents and teachers at "Prospect," a K–5 school in a predominantly low-income White neighborhood in a mid-sized city. She found that "some teachers at Prospect resisted taking on practices of supporting, nurturing, and rearing...which they believed belonged to parents" and reports one teacher as saying that parents should "clean them up, teach them good habits, [and] get them to school on time" (p. 185). Though many of the teachers at Prospect are said to have been "more accepting" of this "additional burden," what becomes clear from the data presented is that these teachers take on this burden grudgingly and only because, as one says, "We can't just turn our backs on these kids" (p. 185). The possibility of forming parent–teacher partnerships at Prospect seems remote. In fact, O'Connor (2001) concludes her study by saying, "If schools are ever to realize true partnerships with parents in the formal education of children, we must dare, in the words of one of the teachers in this study, to 'break the mold'" (p. 197).

Recent studies in Great Britain, however, indicate that differences in parent involvement according to socioeconomic class may begin to decrease. Furlong (2005) reviews the results of two longitudinal surveys and one qualitative study by Glasgow University researchers in Scotland. He reports that though gaps in student participation in education in the 14–19-year age group remain, the past decade has witnessed increased participation for all socioeconomic and ethnic groups at all levels. The Glasgow researchers found that

> the increased emphasis placed on educational attainment in working class families stems, in part, from a growing awareness of the importance of credentials in the modern economy. It can also be linked to a breakdown of a visible dichotomy in the labour market between working class and middle class jobs that has accompanied the decline of manufacturing industry as well as a more educated parentage and a trend towards employment in smaller work units where social divisions are less visible. (p. 380)

The researchers conclude that though "some young people are put in positions at school that effectively promote processes of cultural resistance as survival strategies," "class cultures can no longer be seen as providing significant barriers to educational progression. Indeed...[an] increase in educational participation has been facilitated by a process of cultural convergence" (p. 387). But as working-class families place increased emphasis on the importance of educational achievement, we can also expect them to want to become more involved in their children's school-related activities.

Parent Involvement and Ethnic Background

When scholars try to explain why parents from different ethnic backgrounds are involved in their children's education in different ways, they often look to the legacy of desegregation, a period in the 1970s and 1980s when many low-income African American students were bused to predominantly middle-class White schools in an effort to achieve racial balance and equality of opportunity within school districts. Calabrese (1990), for example, surveyed parents at an elementary school in an upper-middle-class neighborhood in the Midwest in the late 1980s. He found that Black parents at the school were more alienated than White parents because, they said, they were not invited to the school often enough and were contacted only to deal with problems their children encountered; they were frustrated with school policies and procedures they were not involved in making and which were based on White middle-class culture; and the school's White teachers were unfriendly, uncaring, and interacted in negative, confrontational ways. Black parents felt that the school offered little hope to them or their children, and they lacked the knowledge and/or confidence to confront what they perceived to be a large bureaucratic institution. The parents responded by withdrawing from participation altogether, adopting a passive attitude to help their children survive what they perceived to be a hostile environment. But they also feared that their negative attitude toward the school was being transmitted to their children and that this was having a deleterious effect on their children's behavior and academic achievement.

During this same period, studies of parent involvement programs in inner-city schools were demonstrating only limited results. Fine (1993), for example, examined parent involvement programs in Baltimore, Philadelphia, and Chicago. A three-year evaluation of the With and For Parents project in Baltimore showed that though it was intended to reform home–school relations and improve student outcomes, in the end the program mainly served to provide services to needy families and did not improve student retention, absenteeism, grades, and scores on achievement tests. These results led the evaluation team to conclude that "it is not enough for families to become more like schools; schools and districts must also become more like families" (p. 691). The Philadelphia Schools Collaborative placed parents on school-based governance councils, and though "in many schools parents are decision makers working closely with teachers," "in other schools their input is trivialized" (p. 694), leading the team to conclude that "if parents' interests are shaped as private, and schools' interests as 'public,' then a conversation toward a common vision is nearly impossible. Parents (as well as teachers) cannot simply be added to the mix of decision making unless the structures and practices of bureaucracy—school-based and central district—are radically decentralized and democratic" (p. 697).

In Chicago, a major school reform program in the late 1980s had resulted in parents being "positioned as the primary decision makers within schools" (Fine, 1993, p. 700). Though the parents were "intent on importing concerns of culture, class, and community into their schools, as [was] obvious in the rise of interest in African-centered curricula, afterschool programs, and community-service schools" (p. 700), a later study indicated that low-income African American parents still felt alienated from their children's schools (Diamond & Gomez, 2004). In this study, researchers interviewed college-educated, middle-class parents with children at African-centered magnet schools and high school–educated, low-income parents with children at local neighborhood schools. The researchers found that while the middle-class parents were supportive of their quality, diverse schools—ensuring that their children's homework was completed, for example—the low-income parents were critical of their predominantly African American schools and of teachers and administrators, whom they perceived to be defensive and exclusionary.

African American parents today may not be significantly less involved in their children's schools than White parents, but recent studies indicate they are often involved in different ways (Brown & Beckett, in press). According to these studies many middle-class Black parents feel the need to watch over child–teacher relationships, initiate and manage parent–teacher partnerships, form networks with other African American parents, maneuver and customize their children's schooling to gain quality educational experiences in predominantly White schools, choose and actively support quality magnet schools for their children, and organize their communities to take control of their community schools. The main difference between these middle-class Black parents and the middle-class White parents in Lareau's (1987, 2000) study, is that whereas the latter are supportive of what teachers are trying to do in school, believing it to be in the best interests of their children, middle-class Black parents feel the need to intervene with White teachers, administrators, and school district officials to ensure that their children's interests are protected. Thus decades of activism have not just institutionalized a high level of access for African American parents but also determined the goals to be achieved and some of the strategies to be used once access has been gained.

Low-income African American parents, on the other hand, like their working-class White counterparts, are what Diamond and Gomez (2004) call "non-choosers" whose children go to neighborhood schools or are bused to predominantly White schools in middle-class neighborhoods. But even here there is evidence of what might be described as a different form of non-involvement. Though low-income White parents are less involved in their children's education than middle-class White parents, low-income Black parents are not just less involved than middle-class Black parents, they can also feel a "wholesale suspicion, distrust, and hostility" for their children's teachers (Lareau & Horvat, 1999, p. 44) and can in some cases act to undermine the work the teachers are trying to do. Lareau and Horvat (1999) describe Mr. and Mrs. Mason, pastors of a small church, whose daughter Faith is bused to an elementary school in an affluent White neighborhood in a small Midwestern town. While the Masons continually complain that Black students at the school are treated unfairly, they also encourage Faith to use the "race card" against her teachers, and Mrs. Erickson, her English teacher, gives her a higher mark on a test because, as she says, "I just didn't want to have a scene" (p. 44).

Class, Ethnicity, and Language

The theme that emerges from these studies of parent involvement in urban schools is one of schools being "owned" by middle-class White families and mainly serving their interests. But urban schools are also "used" by working-class White families to gain access for their children to post-secondary technical training and by middle-class Black parents to gain access for their children to college and university. Only low-income Black parents would appear to have no use for urban schools at all. Studies of parent involvement in diverse urban schools serving linguistic as well as ethnic minority families confirm the hypothesis that low-income and minority parents place limits on the levels and forms of their involvement. Smrekar and Cohen-Vogel (2001), for example, studied home–school relations at an elementary school in Northern California which served a mixed Black–Hispanic–Pacific Islander community. The researchers report that school officials "suggested that most of the parents in the school were lazy, irresponsible, and apathetic when it came to school involvement and that these attitudes were inextricably linked to the low performance of their children" (pp. 84–85). In interviews with the parents, however, the researchers found that the parents "value education and would like to be more involved, but their involvement is limited by a sense that their roles are distinct from those of schools" (p. 96): "the consistency with which this diverse group of parents regarded two tasks, attendance at meetings and assistance with homework, as encompassing the universe of parental roles was stunning" (pp. 87–88).

Abrams and Gibbs (2000, 2002), to take a second example, analyzed home–school relations at a K–5 school, also in Northern California, serving White, Latino, African American, and some Asian families. Though parents from all of the school's major communities participated at least to some extent in their children's school-related activities, with White parents participating the most, the activities they were involved in and their motivation for participating were significantly different. Affluent, White "hills" parents, who could have sent their children to private schools, were primarily concerned with quality academic programs and with ensuring that their children kept up with their White peers. African American parents took a special interest in programs for students who needed additional support and in ensuring that their children kept up with the White students. Finally, Latino parents were active in support of the school's bilingual programs. These differences in involvement are also seen in relation to the school's parent–teacher association. The association is run by the White parents (one White mother is quoted as saying, "If we…didn't participate, there would be no PTA," p. 391); Latina mothers, believing that the White parents kept power to themselves, formed their own parents' group; and African American parents appear not to be involved at all.

In both of these case studies, low-income and ethnic and linguistic minority parents clearly feel that the schools are not theirs, and they choose to limit their involvement to school programs, groups, meetings, and activities that directly concern their own children. Only the affluent White parents in the second example appear to feel that the school is theirs and that they have a responsibility to provide general support for all of the school's programs.

School Communities That Work

In case studies of urban schools which are successful in building strong ties with the families and communities they serve, the emphasis is on common ownership based on increased communication and shared norms of behavior. In none of these studies, however, do we find ownership crossing socioeconomic or ethnic lines. We have already seen in the work of Lareau (1987, 2000) and Weininger and Lareau (2003) that communications between middle-class teachers and middle-class parents in urban schools indicate common ownership and shared norms. The parents at Swan, for example, are said to use parent–teacher conferences to probe for areas of weakness in their children's academic performance where they might be of help at home, while at the same time feeling free to persist in criticisms of what teachers are doing in the classroom. In both instances, there is an assumed sharing of responsibility and a belief that it is the responsibility of parents to supplement what the teacher is doing and to point out possible unintended consequences of teacher actions on their children. In this section we will show that communications between Black teachers and Black parents in urban schools which have a tradition of service to Black communities also indicate common ownership based on shared norms of behavior.

Morris (1999, 2004) studied two elementary schools serving low-income Black communities in St. Louis and Atlanta, chosen in part because of their high student attendance rates and test scores, high levels of parent involvement, and strong community connections. He describes "Fairmont" Elementary in St. Louis as being embedded in the community it serves: some teachers were born in the community, two still live there, and one teacher is godparent to several current students; some teachers taught the parents of their current students, and some former students who have moved away send their children back to Fairmont; many parents volunteer at the school during the day and between 100 and 150 attend PTA meetings in the evenings; teachers in turn call and visit with families at home on a regular basis. Furthermore, the school is said to have replaced the church as the most important institution in the neighborhood, hosting such activities as scouts, GED classes, after-school child care, and a free clothing program and including news from the community in its student-run newspaper. One nearby resident describes school staff and the school itself as "neighborly, very neighborly" (1999, p. 595).

The schools in St. Louis and Atlanta are said to reach out to and welcome in parents and community members. To illustrate this point, Morris quotes at length from an interview with a recently retired paraprofessional from "Lincoln" Elementary in Atlanta:

> We had this one parent. She had a disability problem, but she could function. That parent came up, she came up about 2 or 3 years, and I'll never forget! She would come in and tell the children stories. And that teacher would find her something to do. And the children got used to it. Her [the parent's] daughter was in that room, and her daughter was very proud that her mama could come up and do something. Because she was very protective, she was just a kindergarten child. I'll never forget it. She was protective of her mother because she knew that she was smarter than her mother. But after her mother came up, and the teacher let her come up and tell stories to the children, that child was real proud. (2004, p. 90)

The success of these schools in building strong home/school/community partnerships does not depend on parents and community members taking active roles in the running of the schools or on learning environments which emphasize a shared African American heritage. Unlike the "[ap]parent" involvement Fine (1993) describes in Philadelphia and Chicago, where parents sit on local school governance councils, the parents and teachers in St. Louis, for example, are said to view their roles as being mutually inclusive, that is, as distinct but overlapping. The overlap occurs because home and school are seen to be parts of a larger community, and as members of that community parents must work to strengthen the school (PTA, volunteering) and teachers must work to strengthen homes (after-school programs, GED classes). Unlike Chicago parents who use their positions as primary decision makers in their local schools to promote African-centered curricula, apart from some of the younger teachers at Lincoln wearing African clothing accented with Kente cloth patterns and a focus on achievement test preparation in an effort to combat published reports highlighting gaps in achievement between middle-class White suburban schools and inner-city Black schools in Atlanta, there seems to be little felt need for cultural affirmation or consciousness raising to play a prominent part in the curriculum of either school. The implicit message is that the communities Lincoln and Fairmont serve are first and foremost communities. The fact that they are also Black communities seems to be taken for granted.

Conclusion

On the basis of the studies reviewed in this chapter it is reasonable to conclude that the support model of parent involvement is not working in urban schools which serve diverse socioeconomic, ethnic, and linguistic communities. But in most cases a partnership model of parent involvement would require a willingness on the part of middle-class White teachers to relinquish some of the authority they have possessed in the past, and this may be difficult. The response of teachers might be analogous to that of the kindergarten student in Shaker Heights, Ohio, upon being told he had not been chosen group leader: "I'm the White boy. This should be my group" (Ogbu, 2003, p. 68). Equally important, however, the partnership model would require a determination on the part of working-class and ethnic and linguistic minority parents to take on responsibilities which in the past many have avoided. It would no longer be acceptable for working-class parents, for example, to adopt "a certain resignation" (Crozier, 1999, p. 312) or to say, as one parent did, that her child's school seemed to be "running itself quite well" (p. 321).

But the studies we have reviewed also indicate that the main issues separating teachers and parents in urban schools are not intractable. Though it is true that teachers would have to recognize that schools must serve different families in different ways, it does not seem to be asking too much of teaching professionals to recognize and value the aims of working-class parents who may not be focused on preparing their children for college, of disadvantaged African American parents whose first concern must be for their children's safety, or of linguistic minority parents who may feel that schools are for their children and their futures but not for them. At the same time, working-class and ethnic and linguistic minority parents must recognize, as many

White parents do, that the ability of their children's school to satisfy their particular family and community needs depends on the strength of the school as a whole. But one of the lessons of the research on parent involvement in the United States is that when schools reach out to low-income and ethnic and linguistic minority parents, the parents often respond positively. It has been found, for example, that the strongest, most consistent predictors of parent involvement are not the socioeconomic, ethnic, or linguistic backgrounds of parents but specific school programs and teacher practices that encourage involvement. Simply put, "when parents believe that schools are doing little to involve them, they report doing little at home. When parents perceive that the school is doing many things to involve them, they are more involved in their children's education at school and at home" (Dauber & Epstein, 1993, p. 61).

Chapter 5

Separate African American Schools: Giving Voice to Silenced Communities

Introduction

SO FAR we have focused on trying to understand some of the challenges faced by middle-class White teachers in increasingly diverse urban classrooms. We have seen that in these classrooms poor Black males are especially at risk for educational failure. What we have not considered so far is the challenge faced by African American students and their families in urban schools increasingly staffed by middle-class White teachers. To do this we must first try to understand a part of our educational history that until recently has been largely forgotten and is only now being re-discovered. Desegregation in the 1960s and 1970s affected White and Black communities differently. For White teachers in previously all-White schools the challenge was to integrate Black students into their classrooms. This was a challenge both personally and professionally, as stereotypes and latent racism came face to face with real kids, and as educational methodologies that had been successful with White students met with increasing resistance from Black students. But the challenge was even greater for Black students and their families, as desegregation had the effect of closing Black schools and bringing to an end a history of separate Black education that can be traced back to slavery and beyond. White teachers had to make adjustments to welcome new students into their classrooms, but Black students, families, and communities had to come to terms with a wholly new White-dominated school system. In this chapter we will describe the relationship between separate Black schools and the families and communities they served, the leadership roles played by Black principals, and the educational methodologies used by Black teachers in segregated schools. Our aims are to provide a context in which to understand the challenges faced by urban schools and the families and communities they serve today, and to point toward a future in which, when we have learned the lessons of the past, these challenges can be met and overcome.

The history of African American education is currently being re-written to remove a form of racism inherent in earlier accounts that emphasized what Black schools lacked when compared with White schools (Brown, Beckett, & Beckett, 2006). Throughout the period of segregation Black schools were funded at about one-quarter the level of White schools. This lack of funding restricted the range of programs that Black schools could offer but did not affect their overall quality. With few other opportunities open to them, most Black college graduates entered the teaching profession, and with their knowledge and professionalism, and their commitment to advancing the race through education, Black teachers were successful in providing their students with a quality education. After desegregation, with the closing of Black schools, the demotion of Black principals, and the firing of Black teachers, Black children and their families were confronted with a situation they had not witnessed since Reconstruction, when the Freedmen's Bureau and Northern philanthropic societies helped establish schools in Black communities in the South and hired Northern White teachers to teach Black children. The difference today is that whereas Black communities in the South after Reconstruction quickly took control of their schools and hired Black college graduates to teach their children, and though some Black communities today are attempting to do something similar by opening independent Black schools, taking control of their community schools, or sending their children to African-centered magnet schools, the vast majority of Black families are doing the best they can to work with predominantly White teachers and school officials to improve the education offered at their neighborhood schools. The issue for us, then, is to apply a form of reverse racism and to ask what White-dominated schools today lack when compared with Black schools in the past. What, if anything, can White teachers and school officials in the era of desegregation learn from the experience of Black communities, principals, and teachers during segregation?

Slavery

The significance that education has for many African Americans and the unique role that educators have traditionally played in Black communities can be traced back to the experience of slavery (Fairclough, 2001; Spring, 2005). We have long known that some slave masters who needed literate personal secretaries and slave drivers allowed their wives or governesses to teach slave children alongside their own children and that in some families later generations of slave children were taught to read and write by their own parents. But we have also known that most slave masters took active steps to prevent their slaves from acquiring literacy and that toward the end of slavery, with Northern philanthropic societies bringing abolitionist literature to the South and opening schools for Blacks, Southern states passed a series of laws making it a crime to educate slaves. What we have not fully appreciated until recently is that a remarkable number of slaves were autodidacts and that some literate slaves were able to establish clandestine schools to teach other slaves. This fact helps us to understand why by the time of Emancipation, and despite increasing White hostility, between 7 and 10% of the Black population was literate.

For many slaves, education meant gaining "a measure of the dignity and power of literacy" (Nolen, 2001, p. 29). Garvin Fields (1983), for example, in her "Carolina memoir," recalls being taught history by her Cousin Lala:

> It was from her that I learned about slavery as our relatives had experienced it and what it meant. She told us about her grandfather, who had gone to England as a valet with the Middleton boys—how he studied right along with them and then taught his own sons, Uncle Abe and Uncle J. B., to read and write English, Hebrew, and Greek....She taught us how strong our ancestors back in slavery were and what fine people they were. I guess today people would say she was teaching us "black history." (p. 45)

For other slaves, however, education was a criminal act. One widow, for example, thinking of her husband and with only half a smile on her face, remembered that "[o]n his dyin' bed he said he been de death o' many a nigger 'cause he taught so many to read and write" (cited in Spring, 2005, p. 114). In either case,

> the efforts of the slave regime to prevent black literacy meant that blacks early on associated education with liberation....The freedmen did not need New England missionaries to teach them the value of literacy: they knew its importance already. Indeed, by 1860 black southerners had attained a degree of literacy remarkable under the circumstances. (Fairclough, 2001, p. 3)

Reconstruction

As mentioned, during Reconstruction the federal Freedmen's Bureau, in cooperation with Northern philanthropic societies, was active in establishing schools for Southern Blacks, especially in the towns and cities, and the Bureau staffed the schools mainly with Northern White teachers. We know that the freedmen schools were successful in attracting large numbers of students, both children and adults. Nolen (2001) hardly exaggerates when he says that "in these early days when education promised to open all avenues to advancement, many blacks had a hunger for knowledge and a dedication to study. Wherever schools were opened the old and young flocked to them" (p. 168). But Butchart (1990) has found that up to 15% of teachers in the early freedmen schools were educated Northern Blacks, participating at rates that were more than 12 times their percentage of the Northern population, and that these Black teachers stayed at the schools on average one and a half times longer than Northern White teachers. The net result was that as early as 1867, more than half of the teachers in freedmen schools were Black.

What we are only beginning to appreciate is that it was Southern Black communities that took the initiative in establishing schools for their children and that they sought assistance from the Freedmen's Bureau only where and when it was needed. Black schools in the South during Reconstruction did not depend solely on the assistance of the Bureau and the Northern philanthropic societies; they were strongly supported by all segments of the Black community. As soon as the Northern White teachers began leaving and as more educated Blacks from all over the country realized the opportunity the schools presented both personally and professionally, Black communities took deliberate steps to hire Black principals and teachers. Butchart (1990) aptly notes that "historians are beginning to realize that the freedmen were central actors in securing their own schooling, not merely passive recipients of northern benevolence" (p. 82). In fact, Black communities were so successful in this crusade for education after the Civil War that by the early 1870s a higher percentage of Southern Black children than of Southern White children were enrolled in school (Spring, 2005).

It is difficult even for professional historians to grasp the magnitude of what Southern Black communities accomplished during this period. Spring (2005) calls it, simply, "one of the greatest educational advancements in the history of education" (p. 192). Harder still, perhaps, is to understand the motivation behind the achievement, but Fairclough (2001) seems to get it right when he says that

> Black southerners subscribed, perhaps more fervently than any other group, to the ideology of the public school advocates that education was democracy's great equalizer. Laboring under a double burden of poverty and discrimination, they expected education to serve double duty as a means of advancing both the individual and the race. Like religion, education provided a means of sustaining hope in an otherwise hopeless situation. (p. 9)

Segregation

After Reconstruction, faced with increasing hostility from Southern White regimes reasserting political, economic, and social control, and with the withdrawal of support from the federal government, Black communities responded with a renewed emphasis on the importance of education, on gaining and maintaining control of their schools, and on hiring Black principals and teachers. This effort culminated in a second crusade for Black education in the South from roughly 1910 to the 1930s that "involved the expansion of segregated schools for African American children paid for by a combination of personal donations of time and money by black citizens, donations by private foundations, and government money" (Spring, 2005, p. 226). Spring (2005) emphasizes the fact that "it was through the struggles and sacrifices of the black community that by the 1930s African American children in the South had a viable system of education," noting that "black southern citizens had to pay directly from their own income to build schools for their children while, at the same time, they paid local and state taxes, which went primarily to support white segregated schools" (p. 227). Nonetheless, "by the 1930s, through these efforts, common schools were finally established for black children" (p. 227).

According to Siddle Walker (2003), Black schools during segregation "became places notable for their exemplary teachers, their curriculum and extracurricular activities, their parental involvement, and the leadership of school principals" (p. 59). With the collapse of Reconstruction blocking opportunities in other directions, under-funded Black schools were able to recruit highly educated Black teachers. By 1910 more than half of all Black college graduates were teachers, and 30 years later a U.S. Census survey of Black professionals counted 1,000 lawyers, 3,500 medical doctors, 17,000 ministers, and 63,000 teachers. As one former student at a segregated Black school recalled, "you have to remember...that for many years—and this was certainly true when I was a child—the teacher was the person in the community....That was because primarily [teaching] was the profession that most blacks went into if they wanted to get ahead and so forth" (Dempsey & Noblit, 1993a, p. 56).

Who were these teachers? How are they remembered today? In Chapter 3 we cited Foster (1993) and Stanford (1998), who interviewed exemplary Black teachers in desegregated schools in the 1980s and 1990s who had attended segregated Black schools in their youth. These teachers described their own "most memorable" teachers as concerned individuals who commanded respect, were respectful of pupils, and who were strict but caring. Siddle Walker (1993, 1996) studied the Caswell County Training School in North Carolina, basing her work in part on interviews with former students. She found that "students were motivated to excel...because they did not want to disappoint those who were working so hard to ensure their success" (1993, p. 73). One former student recalled being asked to spell a difficult word: "I knew I could spell it, yet forgot when I was called on. The teacher looked so disappointed that I remembered. It just came back" (pp. 73–74).

When describing the motivation of Black teachers during segregation, Stanford (1998) used the phrases "lifting as we climb," or racial uplift, and "giving forward," that is, teaching students who would strengthen the community in the future. Garvin Fields (1983) gives an example of a Black teacher giving forward when she says that during Bible reading her Cousin Lala "would interpret, since the language was hard for us...so one day we could be Bible teachers in our church schools" (p. 45). She implicitly contrasts Cousin Lala with the Southern White teachers she later encountered in public school who seemed intent on limiting the contribution their students might make to their communities in the future: "Miss Dixon was supposed to teach history, but I never knew what it was all about. All you did was read and recite....While you recited, she would follow along in the book. If you made a mistake, the cane. And you could never ask a question" (pp. 44–45). Garvin Fields (1983) also gives meaning to the phrase "lifting as we climb." As a young teacher in poor, isolated James Island, South Carolina, she says, "we did our best to teach proud ways to the children" (p. 220):

> If they came to the desk to ask for something, they would shuffle to beg my pardon. Oh, I threatened the children that I would punish them. "You must not do that!" Well, their mother told them to do it. "Mind, I am going to tell your mother too. She

had to do it, but you don't have to do it." Half the time they would come back with "Yes, ma'am," and I had to start all over again, "Say, 'Yes, Mrs. Fields,' Don't ma'am me!" (p. 221)

During segregation Black parents were especially active in supporting their children's schools. On one level, Black parental involvement included "beginning their own schools, using the church and other institutions to promote education, lobbying white school leaders for school reform measures, organizing local meetings and state conventions to plan strategies for improving education, and engaging in a variety of direct protest measures" (Siddle Walker, 2003, p. 67). But on the level of day-to-day school operations, Black parents worked especially closely with teachers to discipline their children. This practice evolved from a tradition in separate Black communities where neighbors were "lifelong friends, free to go into each other's houses at will and encouraged to supervise and discipline each other's children" (Dempsey & Noblit, 1993b, p. 321). Garvin Fields (1983) remembers that Cousin Lala's mother, Aunt Harriet, "used to do what they call 'social work' now. She didn't only take care of the children in our two houses, she took care of all the children around, it seemed. If they didn't do what Aunt Harriet thought they should, she'd whip them good and then tell their mother what they were doing and that she had whipped them" (p. 39). When the family opened a school for Cousin Lala, "Aunt Harriet carried on and served as principal, supervising the children in the yard and helping with discipline" (p. 41). Later at college, majoring in pedagogy, Garvin Fields (1983) found that "whatever else we did, we were advised at all times to keep close to the parents, even if that meant going home with a child after school. The parents would discipline their own children and sometimes even come up to the school to do it. Since the children didn't like that, they behaved" (p. 99).

Siddle Walker (2000) has found that by the 1950s more than 90% of Black principals in North Carolina held masters degrees, making them the most educated people in communities where education, especially advanced education, was highly esteemed. Principals were commonly called "professor" or "fessor." Blacks used the term with respect, even reverence, but Whites used it to avoid saying "Mr." School principals took on leadership roles in their communities, including motivating parents to provide resources for their schools; acting as financial advisors and marital counselors; being active in their churches, often teaching Sunday school; providing leadership for local initiatives like credit unions; and often providing the only link Blacks had with the larger White community. But it was in the school itself that Black principals' leadership roles are best seen:

> Operating with almost complete autonomy and armed with his educational commitment and training, the principal was able to implement a school program in keeping with his philosophy. His autonomy was a direct outgrowth of the neglect of the school board and superintendent and their lack of interest in the achievement in Negro schools. Because of this neglect, the principal held the authority to hire teachers in line with his vision and fire those who did not conform. He held almost complete power over the school program. (Siddle Walker, 2000, p. 275)

As early as the 1930s, however, the preeminent position of teachers and principals in Black communities was being challenged by ministers and lawyers. Historians contrast the position Black educators had achieved within the White power structure with the relative independence of Black ministers and lawyers, who were beginning to question White dominance: "Unlike ministers, they depended upon white support: school improvement had to be achieved through supplication and persuasion rather than negotiation and pressure. Black teachers therefore went to great lengths to obtain white protection and approval" (Fairclough, 2001, pp. 14–15). Black principals came to be seen as symbols of White exploitation and humiliation: "In the towns and cities, white superintendents kept black principals under careful scrutiny, and looked to them as a source of information about what was going on inside the black community. Superintendents and school board members also used them as chauffeurs, gardeners, and repair men, and sometimes treated their wives as washerwomen" (p. 15). At a time when Black ministers and lawyers were beginning to challenge segregated schools as inherently unequal, "the role of teachers as racial diplomats…made it hard for blacks to regard them with unalloyed respect. On the one hand, teachers were admired for their selfless dedication; on the other hand, their lack of militancy, and the privileged status that whites bestowed upon them, rankled" (p. 15).

But Black communities were also aware that state education officials and representatives from Northern philanthropic organizations, however paternalistic, were, "by and large, sincere advocates of black education" (Fairclough, 2001, p. 58), that the civil rights movement would not have been possible without the advances in Black education that had been made since Reconstruction, and that most of the leaders of the movement were themselves graduates of Black schools and colleges. As one historian has said,

> During the grim years of Jim Crow black teachers had to work within the confines of segregation and were unable to furnish overt political leadership. Yet in resisting the basic ideas of white supremacy—racism and inequality—they helped to undermine the Jim Crow regime. By insisting upon the sanctity of knowledge and the innate humanity of black children, they performed political work of the most far-reaching kind. (Fairclough, 2001, p. 67)

Desegregation

The role of educators in Black communities, having reached its zenith around 1930, found its nadir in the period after the U.S. Supreme Court's *Brown v. Board of Education* decision in 1954. This was because "desegregation, or the creation of a unified educational system, took a 'one-way' direction. Rather than a synthesis of the strengths of both black and white schools, desegregation modeled public schooling overwhelmingly on the needs and concerns of European Americans" (Beauboeuf-Lafontant, 1999, 713). Desegregation was done "on white terms" (Dempsey & Noblit, 1993b, p. 319), "disproportionately burdening African-Americans with the bulk of busing, with the closure of African-American schools, and with the demotion and firing of African-American educators" (p. 318). Siddle Walker (2003) found that as a result of desegregation and the closing of Black schools, more than 30,000 Black teachers lost their jobs and Black principals became "almost nonexistent."

After desegregation, Black students increasingly found themselves marginalized in White classrooms. No longer encouraged by Black teachers to succeed against the odds, they seemed expected by White teachers to fail. This change was especially harmful for Black male students. Foster and Peele (1999) say that "effective teachers of African American males believe that…academic achievement results from concerted and consistent effort, not from ability. Consequently, successful teachers of African American males accept responsibility for motivating students" (p. 13). But too many White teachers seemed unable or unwilling to establish the types of relationships with their Black male students that would motivate the students to make this effort. Similarly, after desegregation Black parents found themselves alienated in White-dominated schools. Without the special connection provided by a Black school serving a Black community and the special relationship in which Black parents and teachers raised a community's children together, parents no longer felt able to give schools the sort of support they needed to ensure success. Desegregation, so long sought and so bitterly fought for, was, at least in the short term, what Dempsey and Noblit (1993b) call a form of "cultural genocide" (p. 319).

When school districts began re-hiring Black teachers and re-appointing Black principals in the 1970s and 1980s to serve mainly in under-performing, predominantly Black urban schools, they were tapping into a century-old tradition of African American educational success that depended largely on the work of exemplary Black teachers. But Black teachers were now a minority on predominantly White teaching staffs, and they taught in classrooms which included some White, Hispanic, and Asian students. Desegregation weakened Black teachers' solidarity with Black students and limited their ability to act as "admonishers, urgers, and meddlers," especially with Black male students. In her interviews with exemplary African American teachers, Foster (1990) found that desegregation made it harder for them to conduct the sort of critical dialogue they felt was necessary to engage their students in learning: Why are you here? To better yourself. Who's the competition? The White kid. But to have a chance you have to be better than him. Getting Cs is not good enough. Furthermore, Fordham (2001) says that at Capital High Black teachers were "often perceived to be 'functionaries' of the dominant society" (p. 145) and that "black students' reluctance to embrace the values reflected in school-sanctioned practices undermines their teachers' confidence in their ability to master the prescribed knowledge" (p. 146).

When public school systems began re-hiring Black teachers and re-appointing Black principals in the 1970s and 1980s, their failure to halt overall declines in student attendance, discipline, and achievement opened them to criticism from within Black communities. Speaking of this period, Franklin (1990) says that "the educational achievement levels for Black students and others continued to plunge as dropout (and absentee) rates soared" (p. 59). Implicitly contrasting Black educational leaders with the leaders of the civil rights movement, he criticizes educational leaders because, "despite increased information and research on urban schools and programs that achieved educational success for African American students, Black educators and administrators made no collective commitment to educational revitalization within African American communities" (p. 59). But what this criticism fails to acknowledge is that after desegregation Black educators were no longer accountable solely to Black students, parents, and communities and that the strategies they had employed in segregated Black schools in the past were no longer viable in the more diverse schools of the 1970s and 1980s.

After desegregation, it was the leadership provided by individual Black principals that would prove decisive in re-energizing staff and students at some predominantly Black schools and would begin the long process of revitalization we can now clearly see in Black education generally. Lomotey (1989) conducted case studies of three successful African American principals in predominantly Black elementary schools in California in the early 1980s. He says that "perhaps the most meaningful finding in this study is that there appear to be three qualities that these principals all hold in common. Each principal appears to demonstrate a commitment to the education of African-American children, a compassion for, and understanding of, their students and of the communities in which they work, and a confidence in the ability of African-American children to learn" (p. 132). Lomotey gives examples of how these qualities were demonstrated, especially in the area of student discipline. He says that all three principals were generally focused more on people issues than on money issues; one principal was aware that disciplinary actions "must not only fit the offense...they must also fit the student" (p. 188); and a second principal used what she called an eclectic form of discipline, because, as she explained, if she tried to implement a systematic program such as assertive discipline, "once you set up your rules, three strikes, you're out, and I mean they're out in like 3 minutes, because they're gonna do a number of things to just make your plan totally unworkable" (p. 190).

More recent studies of Black principals' leadership roles within their schools also emphasize their depth of commitment to their students and confidence in their students' ability to learn. These qualities are exhibited either indirectly in the high standards they set for themselves in their own work and which they expect teachers and students to follow in theirs or directly in what Reitzug and Patterson (1998) call "a form of caring that empowered students by assisting them in identifying alternative ways of proceeding as they addressed the situations that confronted them" (p. 165). Case (1997), as we saw in Chapter 3, found an example of this form of caring when Marquerite, the young African American principal in Connecticut, told her about a sixth grader whose father sells drugs and whose mother is a prostitute and how, when the student has a "bad day" she brings him to the office to discuss "what he could have done in this given situation and what he did do in the given situation."

More recent research has also focused on Black principals' understanding of and commitment to their school communities. Bryant (1998), as we noted in Chapter 3, examined an attempt to implement a school reform program under two principals. She found that the second principal was more successful than the first mainly because of his ability to read the surrounding community and his relationship to it and to involve parents and community members in the work of the school. Gooden (2005), to take a second example, examined the role of an African American principal at an urban information technology high school in the Midwest. The principal was himself a graduate of the high school and attended elementary and middle schools in the same neighborhood. Like the principals in Bryant's (1998) study, he was brought in to implement a school reform program: "setting high standards and raising expectations for students were new clearly established and well-articulated goals that he propagated starting his 1st day on the job. He maintained high expectations for everyone in the school, including himself" (p. 638). The principal exhibited "a compassion for and understanding of African American children and their communities as described by Lomotey (1989) [that] can be summed up as being Black is not enough" (p. 644).

Conclusion

Beginning during Reconstruction and continuing through segregation and into the post-Brown era, Black educators have depended for their success on the support of Black parents and other community members. Black parents and community members, in turn, have been focused on the importance of quality education for their children and for their communities. This focus on quality education remains as strong today as it was during and after Reconstruction. In the mid-1990s Public Agenda surveyed 800 Black parents and 800 White parents of public school children (Farkas & Johnson, 1998). They found that Black parents, like their White counterparts, believed that the most important goal for public schools was academic achievement for their children. Black parents, in particular, believed that academic achievement was more important than school desegregation. In fact, these parents used academic success as a criterion for judging the effectiveness of desegregation. Though they thought school desegregation was positive on the whole, they also expressed distrust of affirmative action policies in the hiring of school staff, believing that such policies could result in the best teachers and principals not being hired at their children's schools.

Lomotey's (1989) and other researchers' studies of Black principals, as well as Public Agenda's survey of Black parents, clearly indicate that the success of Black principals today depends, as it did in the past, on their commitment to the education of African American children and an understanding of their students and of the communities they serve, as well as on their ability to demonstrate this understanding and commitment effectively to the parents and community members on whose support their success depends. The question that remains, and the one we hope to answer in the following account of a Black principal at an alternative school serving African American and White students at risk of educational failure in an urban school district in the Midwest in the 1990s, is whether the same commitment and understanding that has served African American principals in separate Black schools since Reconstruction can be successful when Black principals lead the more diverse schools which are common in urban school distracts today.

Chapter 6

Black and White in Cincinnati: Integrated or Quality Education?

Introduction

CINCINNATI GAINED national attention in 2001 when the downtown business foundation was shaken by days of racial unrest that followed the killing of a young Black man by city police (Brown, Beckett, & Beckett, 2006). The unrest was a result of continuing racial inequities in all aspects of public life, including a continuing lack of quality, integrated education in the city's public schools. The picture presented in the research literature on *Brown v. Board of Education* emphasizes the lack of progress made in desegregating the nation's public schools, especially in the north and west. The emphasis in Cincinnati, however, has been significantly different. The key document from the *Brown* era in Cincinnati, the *Bronson* settlement agreement of 1984, speaks of achieving racial balance in the city's public schools but also of improving education in the city's seven low-performing Black schools (Erkins, 2002). And in Smrekar and Goldring's (1999) major study of Cincinnati's magnet school programs, as much emphasis is placed on progress in providing quality education for Black students as is placed on progress in desegregation. In this chapter we trace the history of quality versus integrated education in Cincinnati to provide a context in which to understand the challenges faced by the city's Black community during the *Brown* era. Our aim is to show how the lead author's development and implementation of an alternative school for students at risk for educational failure filled a need for quality education for students not served by the city's magnet school programs.

Segregation in Cincinnati

In his history of the American school, Spring (2005) says that during the first half of the 19th century Black literacy was not a crime in the North as it was in the South, but free Blacks in the North were nonetheless systematically denied equal educational opportunity. In Ohio, for example, the state's Black Laws included a provision preventing local school districts from educating "Negroes" at public expense. Though this provision was not applied consistently across the state, local authorities in Cincinnati collected school taxes from Blacks but banned Black children from attending the city's public schools. When it was criticized for following a policy of taxation without representation, the city decided not to collect school taxes from Blacks and mulattoes. But "when it became abundantly clear that they would not be accepted into the "common" schools, Blacks directed their efforts toward establishing their own schools, under their own control" (Bertaux & Washington, 2005, p. 45). The first private school for Blacks in Cincinnati was opened by Henry Collins in 1825 and lasted a year (Sekou Collins, 2004). The first successful school was opened by Owen Nickens in 1834. The school continued in operation until 1849, when the city finally established its first public school for Blacks. Nickens was among the first teachers the city hired to staff the school.

In the 1850s, Cincinnati resumed collection of school taxes from Blacks and used the revenue to fund a separate Black school system with Black teachers and principals working under a separate school board elected by adult Black males and reporting to the city's board of education. In the following decades up to 1,000 children attended the city's Black schools in a given year, and the schools were staffed by up to 30 teachers and principals, making Cincinnati's Black school system the largest in Ohio. During this period, Ohio's Black schools "were run efficiently and professionally, and serious efforts were made to provide conveniently located schools and a curriculum similar to that available to White students" (Gerber, 1973, p. 4). In Cincinnati, Black teachers were paid slightly more than half what White teachers were paid, well above the national average at the time. As a result, "Cincinnati's black teachers became the first established group of black professionals and the core of an emerging black economic elite" (Bertaux, 1994, p. 42). As Tyack (1974) says in his history of American urban education, before the creation of the black school system, Negroes in Cincinnati had a flat occupational structure: almost all workers were unskilled laborers and servants. With the exception of ministers, most of whom worked at other jobs for survival, there were few who could claim positions of leadership. But with the employment of Negroes as teachers and administrators new career lines opened and new sources of income and prestige appeared....When black Gaines High School opened in 1866, it trained teachers, offered preparation for further education, and helped to create a middle-class leadership for the city's black population. (p. 118)

Though funding for Black schools in Cincinnati was pro-rated and the facilities and equipment provided were a marked improvement over these offered by the pre-1850 private schools, the "physical plants and pedagogical equipment of the Black schools were antiquated and inadequate, and a shortage of teachers hindered the work of the high school" (Gerber, 1973, p. 4). Still, there was "little evidence of continual protest against inequality and ... no evidence of a wide-spread desire for integration" (p. 16):

The racial prejudice of an almost southern community combined with pride in the long established local Black schools, confidence in Black teachers...and relatively open channels of communication between Blacks and White school officials to stem discontent with inequality and the belief in the desirability and practicality of integration. (p. 16)

By the 1880s, however, this perception was beginning to change. To Blacks in Ohio "surveying the failures of the dual school system to provide adequately for their children, no more obvious badge of inferiority could have been worn by Negro education than its inheriting of discarded White schools and equipment" (p. 5). When a majority of Blacks in Cincinnati finally indicated their support for integration at a time when Black voters were seen to hold the balance of power in many races for seats in the state legislature, in 1887 the legislature finally found the votes that were needed to repeal the last of the Black Laws and to desegregate the state's public schools.

In 1887, Cincinnati's board of education adopted a policy of gradual integration: Black elementary schools, re-named branch schools, would remain open and Black teachers and principals would be re-hired. Though the schools were officially open to Black and White children, only Black children were expected to attend:

> The plan worked well in the beginning because Cincinnati Blacks were content to send their children to the old schools. Indeed a month after the start of the 1887–1888 school year, the Cincinnati Superintendent of Schools reported that only 120 Black children had enrolled in schools other than the branches. Explanation by local Blacks of their seemingly contradictory desire for repeal [of the Black Laws] and refusal to integrate focused on a wish to support the Black teachers who had faithfully served their children for many years. (Gerber, 1973, p. 22)

By 1890, however, 80% of Black children in Cincinnati were attending integrated schools and by 1900 only one of the branch schools remained open. Because Black teachers were not allowed to teach White students and Black principals were not allowed to supervise White teachers, by the turn of the century most Black teachers and principals had lost their jobs.

Over the next decades, a combination of increased migration of Blacks from the South and increasing residential segregation by race led Cincinnati to adopt a neighborhood school policy. As a result, by 1930 approximately half of Black students in the city were again being taught in segregated Black schools by Black teachers supervised by Black principals. During this period, Cincinnati, along with Columbus and Dayton, "stand out as relatively prominent employers of black teachers and also as systems which hired a number of black administrators quite disproportionate to those hired in other cities (Tyack, 1974, p. 226). In these cities "there was generally a high degree of conscious segregation of black pupils in separate schools—and normally black teachers were only allowed to teach in these institutions" (p. 226).

Scates (1938) provides us with a snapshot of the 128 Black teachers who taught 4,025 of the district's 11,500 Black students in separate Black schools in 1936–1937. He says that "in a city that is noted for its well trained teachers, it is interesting to find the Negro teachers having even a higher level of training than the white teachers" (p. 144). He also notes that at a time when Black teachers in the country as a whole were being paid at approximately one-quarter the level of White teachers, Black teachers in Cincinnati were being paid more than White teachers. All Cincinnati Public Schools teachers had been on the same salary schedule since 1927, and as salary increments required continuing college course work and Teachers College at the University of Cincinnati was open to Black teachers on the same terms as White teachers, "the result, after ten years, is that Cincinnati appears to have the highest trained teaching staff of any large city in the country, with the Negro teachers more than keeping up their end" (p. 144).

As in earlier periods of its history, Cincinnati's Black community was ambivalent on the issue of quality versus integrated education. The reason for this ambivalence had always been the ability of the city's Black teachers and principals to provide Black children with a quality education despite being forced to use sub-standard equipment and facilities. In a study comparing the scholastic achievement of demographically matched Black students at segregated and mixed schools in 1920–1930, it was found that, "on the whole, the achievements of Cincinnati Negroes educated in the two types of schools are very similar" and that "the segregated schools of Cincinnati are as effective...as are the mixed schools, in their academic training of Negro children" (Crowley, 1938, p. 32).

Desegregation in Cincinnati

By the time of *Brown* in 1954, Cincinnati's board of education had adopted an official policy of integration while at the same time maintaining de facto segregation under its neighborhood school policy: "because virtually all blacks in the city lived in one of a handful of neighborhoods...most blacks attended schools where most of their classmates were also black, despite the district's official policy of integration" (Clotfelter, 2004, p. 19). The school board at this time was also moving more Black students into existing Black schools by gerrymandering school attendance zones, and it was planning to build new schools that would further entrench segregated attendance patterns (Erkins, 2002; Washington, 1984). In response to these actions, the NAACP filed its first desegregation suit in federal court in Cincinnati in 1964. *Tina Deal v. Cincinnati Board of Education* was "an attempt by the plaintiffs to tie discriminatory actions in housing, especially by public officials, to racial separation in schools. The trial brief in the district court presented such evidence, but, despite the strenuous arguments of plaintiff's council...Judge John Peck ruled the evidence inadmissible" (Whitman, 1998, p. 82). The *Deal* decision was a significant event in the history of desegregation in the United States because it "established tough legal standards for evaluating plaintiffs' claims of unconstitutional school segregation in the North" (Dimond, 1985, p. 33). Speaking of later plaintiffs' claims of inequalities resulting from de facto or unintentional segregation, Dimond says that "the Sixth Circuit had already denied that claim as a basis for finding illegal segregation in *Deal v. Cincinnati Board of Education*. The court's ruling...had also held that neighborhood schools gave parents 'free choice' by allowing them to choose the neighborhood in which they lived, but refused to allow plaintiffs to introduce evidence of housing discrimination to rebut that rationale for school segregation" (p. 26).

In 1971 Cincinnati voters elected to the school board a liberal majority consisting of two Blacks and two White liberals. Toward the end of its term of office in the summer of 1973, the board adopted an open enrollment plan for September 1973. But the school board's liberal majority was defeated in the November 1973 elections, and in December 1973 the lame duck board passed a resolution calling for "forced integration by race and socioeconomic class" (Borman & Spring, 1984, p. 64). When the new conservative board took office in January 1974 it rescinded this resolution and replaced it with a "desegregation plan with a primary focus on magnet or alternative schools and voluntary integration" (p. 64). In response to this step, the NAACP filed its second desegregation law suit in May 1974: *Mona Bronson v. Cincinnati Board of Education*. In its negotiations on *Bronson*, the NAACP pressed the school board to accept a mandatory desegregation plan, but after the federal courts accepted magnet schools as a legitimate method of desegregation in 1975 (Goldring & Smrekar, 2000), the board refused to consider any form of mandatory plan. Negotiations between the board and the NAACP moved in and out of court until the parties reached a court-approved settlement in 1984. According to the *Bronson* settlement agreement, the Cincinnati Public Schools were required not only to maintain racially balanced schools, including racially balanced school staffs, and to ensure race-neutral disciplinary practices, but also to improve education overall and to improve education in the district's seven low-achieving Black schools (Erkins, 2002).

From 1975 until the end of the *Bronson* era in the early 1990s, alternative programs flourished in Cincinnati. By 1993–1994, 44 of the city's 85 school sites serving 40% of the school population had some form of magnet program: "this made Cincinnati's proportionately one of the largest magnet school programs in the country" (Taylor & Yu, 1999, p. 22). Though some gains on desegregation in Cincinnati were clearly made using voluntary magnet programs, it is not clear how Cincinnati's voluntary plan compared with voluntary and mandatory plans in other U.S. cities. Smrekar and Goldring (1999) claim that "without compromise and with scant public notice, both St. Louis and Cincinnati use magnets effectively to create racially balanced schools in their respective school districts....The evidence clearly indicates that the court-ordered desegregation guidelines from which these magnet school programs originated have been efficiently and explicitly addressed" (p. 102). Other researchers are less positive. Armor (1995), in his study of mandatory and voluntary desegregation plans in eight cities, found that though Cincinnati was the only city with a voluntary plan where levels of Black–White exposure increased, its value was the lowest of the four voluntary plans, and Watras (1997) goes so far as to argue that "in part because the city used a largely voluntary plan with magnets, the plan increased racial segregation in Cincinnati schools" (p. 280).

Though Cincinnati's board of education was finally found to have complied with the *Bronson* settlement agreement in 1993, it was in compliance not just because it emphasized magnet programs, which served a minority of Black families with higher incomes and higher education levels, but also because it made progress in improving the education offered at its seven low-achieving schools. Even Smrekar and Goldring (1999), who put the most positive interpretation on Cincinnati's efforts at desegregation, concede that "the issue of racial desegregation tends to be muted by more vocal claims among educators and parents regarding magnet program stability, excellence, and instructional innovation" (p. 102). But as important a contribution as Cincinnati's alternative programs made to improving education overall, as well as to the education of Black students enrolled in them, in this chapter we focus on what was happening in the seven low-achieving schools identified in *Bronson* as most in need of improvement.

Growing up Black

The lead author of the present volume was a teacher, vice principal, and principal in the Cincinnati Public Schools throughout the *Bronson* period and by its end was district deputy superintendent acting as compliance officer for the *Bronson* settlement agreement and overseeing the effort to improve the district's seven low-achieving Black schools. For African American principals in Cincinnati during this time, the significance of the *Deal* and *Bronson* suits was not primarily whether they promoted desegregation, though they recognized the educational value of greater staff and student diversity in schools. The importance of these cases was in the opportunities they presented to Black principals to improve the education their schools offered Black students.

The lead author, a Cincinnati native, was the first in his family to graduate high school. He and all of his brothers and sisters now hold college degrees. He attributes this success to the influence of their grandmother, who raised them in and from poverty, and to her traditional belief in the value of education. He describes his grandmother as a "giving" person, but as Dillard (1995) says of another Black principal raised during the civil rights era, to be born "young, gifted, and Black" at this time was to grow up knowing that "to whom much is given, much is expected" (p. 547). The lead author, who attended both mixed elementary and high schools, remembers having had only one Black teacher during all of his school years. At his college prep school, Walnut Hills, which he entered after writing a competitive examination, most of his classmates were White. Though he had to work several part-time jobs to help his grandmother and his brothers and sisters, he knew that his main focus, which was reinforced at home as well as at school, was to acquire a solid grounding in academic subjects.

The lead author was an undergraduate student in design, architecture, and art at the University of Cincinnati (UC) in 1964 when the NAACP filed the *Tina Deal v. Board of Education* case. This widely publicized and hotly debated civil rights case heightened his awareness of discriminatory practices at UC, especially the university's failure to recruit Black faculty and students. As president of the undergraduate chapter of Kappa Alpha Psi, a Black fraternity, he initiated a dialogue with the president's office that resulted in steps being taken to remove barriers to attracting Black faculty and students to the university. He had graduated from UC with degrees in art and art education and was entering the Cincinnati Public Schools as an elementary school art teacher when the *Deal* suit was dismissed for the last time in 1969. As he established himself in the city's education system, his commitments began to change: from student activist committed to desegregation, he became an educator committed to providing his students with a quality education, first as a teacher and then as a school administrator.

A School Principal

By 1981, seven years after the *Bronson* suit was first brought to court but still three years before the case was settled, the lead author had become principal of Bloom Junior High School, a Black school in the city's basin area (Brown, Beckett, & Beckett, 2006). At this time, Bloom enrolled 500 Black students and 1 White student. The school fulfilled every White racist's dream—and every Black parent's nightmare. Bloom was at the bottom of every category used by the district to assess school performance, including attendance and discipline: average daily student attendance was 59%;

students fought on the way to and from school and throughout the school day, and three teachers were physically assaulted in one year; average annual maintenance costs linked directly to student vandalism were estimated to be $35,000 (a water fountain installed one morning had been kicked from the wall before lunch); and student suspensions and expulsions averaged 400 per year.

It quickly became apparent to the lead author that most of Bloom's predominantly White teaching staff had stopped teaching and acted as if they no longer believed their students could learn: average daily staff attendance was 69%; a review of the few available lesson plans showed that teachers made extensive use of work sheets and showed a lot of films; scores on the California Achievement Test were the lowest in the district; and only 15 students were on the honor roll. Bloom's student enrollment was declining rapidly as parents transferred their children to other district schools and to private schools in the city. In 1981, the lead author was hired as principal and charged by central administration to put a lid on Bloom until it could be closed the following year. With so little expected of him, however, and knowing where his students were coming from because he and his family had been there when he was a student, the lead author felt empowered. Like a Black principal during segregation whose "autonomy was a direct outgrowth of the neglect of the school board and superintendent and their lack of interest in the achievement in Negro schools" (Siddle Walker, 2000, p. 275), the lead author was being given the freedom to do whatever he believed to be best for his students.

By the end of his four-year tenure at Bloom, enrollment had increased from 500 to 600 students, with White enrollment increasing from 1 to 60 students. Average daily student attendance had improved from 59% to 94%. Suspensions and expulsions declined from 400 students in 1981 to fewer than 100 students in 1985. Bloom's student achievement test scores rose from the lowest to the middle grouping of all district junior high schools. The number of honor roll students increased from 15 to 150. Like the students in Morris's (1999, 2004) case studies, students at Bloom were following the example set by teachers who now believed students were capable of learning and who were acting with a renewed sense of professionalism. During the lead author's tenure at Bloom, average daily staff attendance increased from 69% to 97%. Work sheets and films were replaced by rigorous new academic programs. A school that was the worst in its district now received national attention as a high-performing school ("Bloom comes to life," 1981).

The significance of the lead author's success at Bloom lies in the methods he used to achieve it. To transform an almost exclusively Black school without the benefit of an alternative program, he clearly recognized the need to mobilize the entire school community, beginning with its teachers and students. When he first arrived at Bloom, he asked teachers to use their training and experience to work with him to develop specific programs that would help students achieve. He formed teacher teams by grade level and used effective teachers as examples to create tension among teachers who were less effective. As more teachers began to move to the performing group, he used this movement as an opportunity to work with them to develop quality programs such as reading in the content areas and journal writing. He then initiated a second cycle of reform by re-organizing grade levels using the school-within-a-school concept. Teachers agreed that these new strategies and structures helped them to boost student achievement. The lead author capitalized on this agreement to suggest another cycle of reform in the academic program, and together he and the teacher teams implemented a college readiness program at all three grade levels.

Behind all of this work with Bloom staff lay the firm conviction that Bloom students could and would learn. In fact, the motivation to work so closely with teachers on the three reform cycles was not so much the reforms themselves, as important as these were, but the opportunity the work gave him to communicate his conviction to Bloom's teachers. This conviction was first communicated to students at an orientation session held when students returned from spring break in 1981. At this session, the new principal set out clear standards for discipline and high expectations for student achievement. He placed all 500 students on a daily progress sheet that had to be signed by a parent and that he checked personally and signed each morning before students were admitted to school. During the remainder of the school year, the new principal was visible in the hallways, in the cafeteria, and on the playground. He visited classrooms up to three times a period. Wherever students turned, the principal was there to remind them that more was being expected of them.

With the teacher teams, the lead author reached out to parents and other community members. He and the teams held parent conferences when students violated any of the school's 14 "cardinal" rules. He wanted parents to know that the school's expectations for their children's behavior were being raised and that he needed their active support if the school was to be successful. Proactive interventions such as these helped to renew confidence in the school among parents and other community members. Like a Black principal during segregation, the lead author capitalized on this renewed confidence to invite volunteers from the community to provide tutorial and mentoring services for students and to donate books, other materials, equipment, and money to support the reform efforts of the school. In return, the lead author and teacher teams formed structures that promoted student service to senior members of the community.

Perhaps the clearest indication that a transformation was taking place at Bloom came when teachers sponsored their first honor roll assembly. They believed that the students would appreciate the principal inviting distinguished Bloom graduates to talk with them about the ingredients of success. Also, parents and community members indicated that for the first time they felt they had in their new principal a listening ear and an effective advocate. Because of the promising performance of staff and students, they began to ask whether they could do more for the school. Discussions with parents and community leaders led to the formation of an advocacy group, the Coalition for Quality Education in the West End. The coalition successfully petitioned central office administration, and the school board chose not to close the school. Though the lead author was given some of the credit for Bloom's transformation ("America's toughest principal?" 1983), he preferred to see his service at Bloom as one principal's contribution to the district's effort to satisfy the terms of the *Bronson* settlement agreement, as those terms were being developed and finalized during his tenure.

The lead author achieved similar results in his next school assignment. In 1985 he was appointed principal of Withrow Senior High School, returning to the school where he had graduated in 1963. Enrollment at Withrow in 1985 was 2,500 students, 95% of whom were Black. The challenge, as the lead author saw it, was to transform a large Black high school of underachievement into a school of excellence where Black, White, and Asian staff, students, and parents felt welcome, safe, and proud. The focus of his work at Withrow was on initiating, developing, and implementing a broad range of new programs, including an international baccalaureate school, an international studies program, a vocational school, the College Pursuit Magnet Program, and a health and wellness program. His overall approach was to expand course offerings, create a more welcoming environment, and build community outreach programs and partnerships. With this approach, Withrow soon acquired a reputation for excellence ("Principal gets firm grip on Withrow," 1986), and during the lead author's four-year tenure as principal the student population became more diverse, going from 5% White to 20% White and Asian. Again, the lead author saw his service at Withrow as his contribution to satisfying the terms of the *Bronson* settlement agreement by improving education overall and improving racial balance.

Like the principals in Lomotey's (1989, 1990) studies in California at this time, the lead author was able to demonstrate to Bloom and Withrow staff, students, parents, and community members in Cincinnati his commitment to the education of African American children, his confidence in the ability of Black children to learn, and his understanding of his students and his school communities. Also, like the second principal in Bryant's (1998) study of the implementation of a school reform program at an elementary school in California, the lead author was able to read correctly the surrounding communities and his relationship to them. Most important, he knew that for the parents of his students, like the African American parents surveyed by Public Agenda (Farkas & Johnson, 1998), the most important goal he must work toward was academic success for his students. Siddle Walker (1996) reminds us that the saying "it takes a village to raise a child" is of African origin. The lead author recognized that at Bloom and Withrow it would not be sufficient to refocus the energies of staff and students on the goal of academic achievement. Any demonstration of committed and effective leadership had to serve as a means of involving parents and community members in the work of the schools. If he failed in this area, he felt, the gains students and staff made would not be sustained, nor would they form the basis for further improvement in the future, and he would have failed to live up to the expectations of a community that had given so much to him.

Conclusion

In this chapter we have given an account of the lead author's leadership at two of Cincinnati's low-achieving Black schools in the 1980s, placing the account within the larger context of the history of integrated versus quality education in the city's Black community. For the lead author, turning around Bloom and Withrow meant creating structures within which exemplary teachers could act as models for other teachers and, as the teaching staff was transformed, programs within which committed, hard-working teachers could act as models for increasingly committed and hard-working students whose success would encourage parents and community members to become more involved in the day-to-day operation of the schools. As a school principal, the lead author's first commitment was to increasing his schools' capacity to offer students a quality education. When the successes the schools achieved encouraged increasing numbers of White parents to enroll their children at Bloom and Withrow, contributing to the school district's effort to achieve greater racial balance in its schools, for a principal this could be a matter only of secondary importance.

At Bloom and Withrow in the 1980s the lead author worked with teachers, students, parents, and community members to create disciplined learning environments in which student behavior and academic achievement would improve. Though the vast majority of students responded positively to these efforts, the lead author was aware that a minority of students resisted the new regimes and were becoming increasingly isolated, alienated, and disruptive in schools which seemed to be leaving them behind. It was during his tenure at Bloom and Withrow that the lead author first conceived the idea of creating an alternative school for students at risk of educational failure. As we will see in the next chapter, it was an idea he was able to act on in the 1990s when he became deputy superintendent and was given responsibility for student discipline in the district as a whole.

Chapter 7

Project Succeed Academy:
An Alternative School Community

Introduction

WE BEGAN this book by saying that in the popular imagination alternative schools for at-risk students include students who behave badly, teachers who do not care, parents who are not involved, and district officials who are not supportive. We also said, however, that this is a view held by regular school students who look down on (and fear) at-risk students, teachers who have given up on them, parents whose only involvement is to attend entrance and exit meetings, and district officials whose only concern is how well the students perform when they return to their regular schools. For educators committed to alternative forms of education for at-risk students the picture is different. From their perspective, the policies, programs, and practices of regular schools place some students at increased risk for educational failure. These are students whom other students may shun, who do not always respond well to teachers' attempts to instruct and discipline them, who may be neglected by their parents and guardians, and whose performance on achievement tests may bring down school and district averages. But suppose, alternative educators ask, school districts should decide to create educational environments specifically designed to meet the needs of at-risk students: what might they look like? From what we have said so far, they would ideally be separate facilities where all students feel they belong, where teachers are committed to helping students learn, where parents and community members are actively involved in all aspects of the schools' operations, and where district officials are prepared to provide the extra resources that all alternative schools need to succeed.

In Cincinnati in the 1990s a rare combination of circumstances led the city's public school district to try an experiment in alternative education for at-risk students. After decades of White flight to the suburbs and to the city's private schools, after numerous failed school tax levies (voters rejected 10 of 14 levies between 1966 and 1979, including six in a row between 1972 and 1979), after years of declining achievement test scores and increasing levels of disruptive behavior, with Blacks students under-performing and being suspended and expelled at twice the rate of White students, and "while teacher union officials blamed the discipline problem on parents in low-income homes," the fact that "some schools consisting entirely of disadvantaged children had high achievement rates and few suspensions or expulsions" suggested that "the key variable [was] not the student's socioeconomic status but rather the ability of principals and teachers to establish an orderly environment for learning" (Taylor & Yu, 1999, p. 23). A crisis in confidence pervaded a once-proud public school system. This was a public school system whose spirit was once said to be best expressed in the words "co-operation" and "progressivism" (Nearing, 1915/1969) and which at one time had led the nation in responding to the needs of linguistic, socioeconomic, and ethnic minority communities (Tyack, 1974).

Background

In the early 1990s, the Cincinnati Public Schools faced what was widely perceived to be a crisis in student discipline (Brown & Beckett, 2006). Many teachers in the district traced the root of the problem to a school board decision in 1988 to ban the use of corporal punishment. When surveyed by their federation in 1989 and again in 1990, more than 90% of Cincinnati teachers reported that disciplinary problems in their classrooms were disrupting instruction and 16% of teachers said they had been attacked by a student in the past year. The apparent inability of district officials to respond effectively to the crisis led to the school board hiring a new superintendent who promised to get tough with disruptive students. But though the new superintendent's disciplinary policies, which had been worked out with the teachers federation as part of a contract agreement, were effective in solving the immediate crisis, they also created a new crisis: student suspensions soared, going from 11,686 in 1990–1991 to 20,594 in 1991–1992, and under new state regulations expulsions now involved students being removed from school for up to 80 days at a time.

Cincinnati's crisis in student discipline was now seen to be so severe that it began to attract attention from civic leaders. In 1991, the Buenger Report, an inventory of the school district conducted by local business leaders, pointed to student discipline as an area of serious concern (Buenger, 1991). In 1992, a mayor's summit on education, discipline, and truancy recommended that the district find ways other than suspension and expulsion to address the needs of disruptive students. In 1993, an external evaluation by Junious Williams found CPS suspensions and expulsions to be too high but could not determine the causes or make specific recommendations for improvement (Junious Williams, 1993). The crisis in student discipline was brought to a head when, in response to these reports advocating reduced use of suspension and expulsion, the federation of teachers adopted a policy of zero tolerance for student misconduct—any infraction not handled properly was to be reported to the union representative for follow-up with the principal. If the district could not provide principals with alternatives to suspension and expulsion they would have no choice but to suspend and expel even more students.

The new superintendent's discipline policies also exacerbated long-standing gaps in the suspension and expulsion rates of Black and White students. In 1991, a federal court, meeting to determine whether the district had satisfied the terms of the 1984 *Bronson* settlement agreement with the NAACP, found the district's efforts to provide race-neutral disciplinary practices and to improve education at its seven low-achieving schools insufficient. In his 1993 external evaluation, Junious Williams reported that, though the data provided by the district prevented him from determining whether the disproportionate suspension and expulsion of Black students was the result of racial bias or higher rates of poverty, he was able to find that the district was more responsive in dealing with issues such as smoking and drug use, which were the main causes of White student suspension, than in dealing with the issue of fighting, which was the main cause of Black student suspension (Bradley, 1994). Williams' report encouraged a local congress of inner-city ministers, the Baptist Minister's Conference, to become active on the issue of racial disparities in student suspensions and expulsions. In 1993, at a time when the district's finances were also in a state of crisis, the ministers openly opposed and campaigned against a proposed school tax levy as a protest against the high rate of suspensions and expulsions among Black students and were widely seen to be effective in helping defeat the levy. Any attempt by the district to reduce overall suspension and expulsion rates would now also have to deal with the issue of narrowing the disparities in the suspension and expulsion rates of White and Black students.

It was in this context that the school board approved the creation of a district office of student discipline and charged it with the task of developing new discipline policies and programs that would reduce overall suspension and expulsion rates, narrow the gaps in the suspension and expulsion of Black and White students, and provide additional social and academic support for students at its seven low-achieving schools and for chronically disruptive students at all district schools. The district formally recognized the connection between these issues when it appointed the lead author of the present volume director of the office of student discipline and internal compliance officer for the *Bronson* settlement agreement. The lead author was asked to develop and implement a new district-wide code of student behavior that would reduce suspension and expulsion rates overall and narrow the gaps in the suspension and expulsion rates of White and Black students by introducing new policies and programs designed to meet the social and academic needs of the district's most severely disruptive students. The crisis that was occurring in Cincinnati's public schools in the early 1990s caught the attention of the national press and was neatly summarized by a *Time* magazine journalist:

> In 1991 the [teachers] union pushed the CPS to impose a tough new discipline policy, which included mandatory suspension for fighting, forgery, fraud and profanity. Suspensions promptly jumped 77%. In the 1991–1992 school year, more than 10,000 students—20% of the total enrollment—were suspended from school. Many parents were infuriated, complaining, correctly, that the new policies only increased the racial discipline gap. Concedes [superintendent] Brandt: "We had people being suspended for looking at someone the wrong way." Pressured by parents, the district changed course again last fall and enacted a progressive code, which offers more options short of suspension, including in-school detention. Yet the nettlesome racial disparity persists, along with the smoldering debate over whether black students are getting fair treatment. (Hull, 1994, pp. 30–31)

Project Succeed Academy (PSA) was developed and implemented in conjunction with the new district-wide code of behavior. Under the code, regular school principals could recommend that their most severely disruptive students be transferred to PSA. But the approach to student discipline later associated with Project Succeed, which provided principals with a range of pre-suspension options, had been the philosophy guiding the development of the new code of behavior from its beginning. Under the code, schools with large numbers of at-risk students were given additional district support if they chose to implement pre-suspension programs. Together, PSA and the new code of behavior succeeded in achieving their aims. First, on the basis of progress made in developing and implementing the new district-wide code of behavior, CPS was found to be in compliance with the *Bronson* settlement agreement in 1993. Second, in the period 1996–1998, the first two years of full implementation, PSA and the new code of behavior helped reduce district non-mandatory suspensions by an average of 17% and district expulsions by an average of 11.5% per year. In addition, Project Succeed Academy was successful in fulfilling its mission of providing appropriate educational programs for at-risk elementary and middle school students. First, student attendance and parent involvement were unusually high for an alternative school serving this population: student attendance averaged 94.5%, and parent involvement averaged 91% in the school's first two years. Second, the promotion rate of PSA "graduates" returning to their regular schools was also unusually high, averaging 89% in the school's first two years. The district-wide code of behavior is still in existence today. Though modified over the years in response to changes in the structure of K–8 schools in the district and in state and federal laws and to respond better to an increase in gang violence since the plan's inception, the code still emphasizes the importance of reducing suspension and expulsion rates by developing and implementing effective pre-suspension programs.

Overview

In 1993, a summer school principal in Cincinnati called his district's office of student discipline to report that he was going to expel a student for severely disruptive behavior (Brown, 2004). Subsequently, in the fall, the student was assigned to the 5th grade for the third time. In an interview with the director of the office of student discipline, the student revealed what appeared to be the cause of his behavior: he was illiterate and rather than reveal this fact to his classmates he acted out. This incident led the director to request an assessment of the reading levels of all students at the eight summer school sites in 1993. The assessment revealed that 120 of the 1,200 students were functionally illiterate. At the same time, the director became aware of a teacher in the district who "saw that one of her kids wasn't reading by the end of the year; she took it upon herself to work with him in the summer and by the end he was reading" (Gordon, 1998, p. 423). These events were the catalyst for the development of Project Succeed, a comprehensive new approach by the office of student discipline to educating elementary and middle school students who were at risk of educational failure.

Project Succeed began in 1994 as a summer reading program for 200 chronically disruptive K–8 students. As a measure of the program's success that summer, when these first students were invited to continue with the Project Succeed program on Saturdays during the following school year almost all of them signed up. As a program director explained at the time,

> There is a difference in the environment and expectations between regular school and Saturday School. Students who are dropped off at regular school at the front door and walk out the back door, actually come and participate in Saturday School. For some this may mean taking two or three buses to get here and you must remember we begin at 8.30am. We don't provide transportation, but they come. (Gordon, 1998, p. 423)

The summer program was expanded to include 300 students in 1995, and again almost all of these students attended the Saturday program in the following school year. In August 1996, Project Succeed was expanded yet again, this time to include a year-round, stand-alone school housed in its own building and with its own teaching staff. When the Cincinnati board of education announced that a year-round Project Succeed Academy would open in the fall the parent of a boy who had attended the summer and Saturday programs wrote to a local newspaper saying that she "couldn't have been happier":

> My son Michael...entered the program at age 12 with very low self-esteem. It seemed what he needed was exactly what the academy could provide him—one-on-one guidance and an impressive network of people who cared....The transformation in him during the past few years has been truly wonderful. I am proud of him and the fact that he has developed into a responsible young man who cares about himself and others. ("Project Succeed Academy," 1996, p. 20A)

Project Succeed Academy enrolled 300 students in 1996–1997 and 400 students in 1997–1998. In 1997, the school received a state-wide award for excellence ("Top award for Project Succeed," 1997). By 2000, the waiting list of students applying to attend Project Succeed Academy had grown to 800.

After several rounds of budget cuts in the late 1990s, however, the stand-alone academy was closed in 2000. Though the year-round program continued for several years in two regular schools under the leadership of an executive director, Project Succeed was finally ended in 2005. We noted in Chapter 1 that alternative schools for at-risk students have yet to prove they are politically viable: though student behavior and academic achievement often improve in remedial schools, when these improvements are not sustained when students return to their regular schools, school districts "typically conclude that the programs have failed to bring about the improvements sought—rarely, if ever, that the students involved can succeed in an alternative school environment. Thus evidence that supports the need for such variants is often read as testimony to their failure" (Raywid, 1995, pp. 128–129). But in Cincinnati, just as it took a rare combination of circumstances in the early 1990s for the school district to launch its experiment in alternative education for at-risk students, in the late 1990s it took a second combination of circumstances to bring the experiment to an end.

In 1998 Project Succeed Academy lost its founder and foremost champion within the district when the lead author stepped down as acting principal and a permanent principal was appointed. In 1999, when the lead author left the district, a new deputy superintendent with responsibility for student discipline requested an internal evaluation of the academy. At this time, PSA enrollment was in sharp decline as a result of changes in the district's school funding formula that encouraged regular school principals to retain their most disruptive students. Though hundreds of students remained on PSA's waiting list, this was in part because Project Succeed students were being kept at the school for up to two years instead of the six months that had been anticipated when the school opened. Most important, however, after reviewing discipline data, proficiency test scores, and other performance indicators, the Ohio Department of Education refused to renew a special waiver which had allowed the district to use additional Title I monies to support the school's low student–teacher ratio. When the evaluation requested by the new deputy superintendent found that PSA students' levels of academic achievement and suspension and expulsion rates returned to pre-PSA levels when they returned to their regular schools, the deputy superintendent recommended that PSA receive no further additional district funding and that the stand-alone school be closed.

Project Succeed Academy

Aims

The general aim of Project Succeed was to break the causal connections between academic failure, disengagement, restlessness, and disruptive behavior with intensive individual and small-group instruction intended to improve students' academic and social skills. Project Succeed goals were at first limited to assessing students' reading skills and, recognizing the connection between poor reading skills and problem behavior, implementing summer and Saturday programs to bring reading up to grade level, while at the same time working with students and parents on other causes of disruptive behavior. The concern was not just that academic difficulties caused "disengagement, increased frustration and lower self-esteem, which then cause a child to act out" (Arnold et al., 1999, p. 591) but that behavior problems arising outside school resulted in "noncompliance, elevated activity levels, and poor attention, which limit children's academic development" (p. 591). But the issue for Project Succeed soon became whether a summer reading program, however successful, was a sufficient response to the problems faced by elementary and middle school students at risk of educational failure. It quickly became apparent to the lead author that only a more holistic approach could address the needs of PSA students and that this could be accomplished only in a year-long, stand-alone Project Succeed Academy.

Project Succeed Academy was intended to have what Gottfredson (2001) calls a communal social organization:

> Communal schools are characterized by a system of shared values among members of the organization, particularly related to the purpose of the institution, expectations for learning and behavior, and expectations for student achievement; meaningful social interactions among school members; and a distinctive pattern of social relations embodying an "ethos of caring" and involving collegial relations among adults in the institution. They also include expanded roles for teachers so that they are responsible for fostering positive social as well as cognitive outcomes for students. (pp. 85–86)

In contrast to other alternative schools described in the literature, Project Succeed would "create a strong normative climate inconsistent with delinquent norms....Such communal social organizations not only weaken delinquent peer norms, but they also build social bonds (beliefs in conventional rules, attachment to school, and commitment to education) and

An Alternative School Community

learning" (p. 86). Finally, Project Succeed would test the hypothesis that "increased interaction with adults in a caring role also teaches youths self-control" (p. 86).

The PSA Community

Project Succeed Academy was a diverse school community, reflecting in its socioeconomic and ethnic makeup the school district as a whole. The professional staff included teachers who were predominantly White and instructional assistants and case managers who were predominantly Black. School admission policies ensured that the school's student demographics reflected general student demographics in the district. After students were referred to PSA by their regular school principals, "a committee selected possible enrollees based upon their discipline records, race, gender and grade level. Efforts were made to keep the school racially balanced based upon district percentages" (Henderson-Frye, 1999, p. 63). Approximately 60% of PSA students were Black and close to 40% were White. The majority of the White students were working-class students from Cincinnati's many urban Appalachian communities. Some parents sought special admission for their children, but "these were children who did not meet the profile and whose parents saw The Academy as a 'cure-all' even for problems that occurred in the home. These requests were usually denied" (p. 63).

The Project Succeed community was based on a contract signed by students, parents, and the acting principal. Though recommended to Project Succeed by their regular school principals, PSA students, like students in other alternative schools, were admitted only after they and their parents were interviewed by school staff and found to be suitable candidates. The contract outlined what was required of the family to achieve success at PSA and what PSA was required to do to support the family. A case manager assisted in developing the contract and held students, parents, and PSA staff accountable for adhering to the program it prescribed.

All alternative schools for at-risk students feature low student–teacher ratios and small class sizes. Project Succeed Academy was no exception. In 1996–1997, when PSA enrolled 300 students, the teaching staff consisted of 2 teachers-in-charge and 27 classroom teachers. Unlike other alternative schools, however, PSA also featured a low student–*adult* ratio. In 1996–1997, school staff also included 7 substitute teachers who reported to school daily, 27 full-time instructional assistants, a Bushido martial arts specialist, an intervention specialist, and 12 case managers. Other adults in the building daily included the volunteer doctors and nurses who staffed the school's health and wellness program and the parent and community volunteers who were a constant presence in classrooms and throughout the school. When a researcher entered the school's first building, an old elementary school in an economically diverse riverfront neighborhood, she made a mental note of its granite steps, carved ceilings, and Rookwood pottery drinking fountains, its large mural of famous African Americans and eight-foot by nine-foot poster of Martin Luther King Jr., and its clean and quiet hallways (Henderson-Frye, 1999). But the researcher was an experienced teacher and administrator in Cincinnati's public schools, and what she particularly noticed on this first visit was a child "being accompanied through the hall by an adult to get a drink of water" (p. 59). What she may not have known at the time was that PSA students "routinely are escorted by an adult who keeps a hand on a shoulder or a grip on a wrist because many easily lose control and 'go off' in hallways" (Griggs, 1998, p. 1A).

In any large urban district in the United States there is no shortage of qualified and experienced teachers who have a proven commitment to and success in teaching at-risk students. The challenge is to find teachers who are able and willing to work in an alternative school community where they share responsibility with other adults for helping students develop academically and socially. The lead author of the present volume, like principals of Black schools during segregation, was in a position "to hire teachers in line with his vision" (Siddle Walker, 2000, p. 275), and he "made the final selection of the staff through an interview process" (Henderson-Frye, 1999, p. 62). Whom did he select? Mrs. Peters, a teacher with ten years' experience in the school district, describes her relationship with her students:

> I have an attitude that they're gonna succeed. I try to shower that upon them....I will not accept a child not trying....Kids will go as high as you expect them to go. ... I like structure. I feel a lot of these kids come from unstructured backgrounds....They like consistency....They are not mean kids. They have a lot, too much, going on in their heads. They really can't focus on the class work. So much is troubling them....Let me tell you they are not darlings. They are not devils....They can go either way. They can be saved or lost....I think our kids are very unique. I love 'em! (Henderson-Frye, 1999, from pp. 84–87)

Mrs. Evans, a teacher-in-charge with 27 years of experience in the region, is asked what good teaching looks like at Project Succeed:

An Alternative School Community

> If I walked into the classroom, I wouldn't necessarily look for the class to be totally quiet but under control. Students would be learning, giving feedback. There might be a few out of their seats, but they'd be responding to the teacher in a positive manner. (p. 92)

Asked whether the program as a whole was successful, Mrs. Evans says, "Yes. I would say this is an effective program. We've been able to turn a lot of our students around. These children have overcome some real barriers" (p. 92):

> The students get along fine with the staff. Students know when you care and when you are phony. It's just that simple. I think the kids treat us like we treat them....The kids get along fine [with each other]. We aren't having any racial problems. I'm not saying we never have problems because we do....Some days the kids fight, some days they don't. One day the kids are friends, and the next day, they can't bear to be near each other. (p. 91)

PSA teachers recognized and appreciated the support they received from instructional assistants, case managers, parents, and community members. They also recognized, however, that there was an important difference between PSA and regular schools in the way education for at-risk students was conceived and organized and important differences in the roles they and other adults played in the alternative school. PSA was not a school where students came ready to learn and where teachers could focus on teaching and instructional assistants, case managers, parents, and community members could focus on supporting teachers. To satisfy students' immediate needs, all adults became equal partners in providing students with parental support at home and at school. When asked about the strengths of the PSA program, Mrs. Peters said, "The kids come with a lot of issues; we have a lot of ways of working with them with their issues. It's not just a regular classroom where you have just the teacher....The kids constantly get bombarded with people who are going to help them" (Henderson-Frye, 1999, pp. 83–84). Mrs. Evans explained that "if you search the families' background of some of our children, you will find teenage pregnancy, drug addiction, and dropout. Many of our kids are products of these circumstances" (p. 90). But "if someone is having a problem, all of us are there to offer our shoulders, our help" (p. 91).

Alternative schools' primary response to students' disruptive behavior is increased adult presence (Raywid, 1994b, 1995). Increased adult presence provides increased supervision for many working-class students who spend their evenings and weekends largely on their own and who have been taught by their parents to stand up for themselves. Lower Price Hill, one of Cincinnati's Appalachian communities, has been studied extensively. Researchers have found that "the transition from the interdependence of family members that characterizes life in rural Appalachia has not necessarily been made in the urban Appalachian context" (Borman & Stegelin, 1994, p. 177). They found, for example, many young, single welfare mothers moving from apartment to apartment, pursued by social workers, while their sons spent most of their time on the streets in gangs. For Susan Murphy, a teacher in the local elementary school, "all of these women…were deeply caring but did not know what do to for the kids. They had no control…could not make them come in at night…could not make them get up and come to school. The sons were more or less running their own show" (p. 177).

Increased adult presence also provides increased security for many African American students raised in areas with high levels of crime and violence by parents who are more directive and controlling. A researcher found that Project Succeed parents "wanted constant and consistent discipline for their children. Few public school teachers, in their view, provided either the constant careful supervision of their children or the fair and consistent implementation of discipline they so desired" (Gordon, 1998, p. 426). At PSA, however, the aim was to provide just this type of discipline. When interviewed, a PSA case manager said that the school operated on the assumption that

> there are cultural differences in people. Different behavior requires different discipline. Blacks need a more stern hand, more structure. Can't let them dilly dally. Some Whites think that what a Black kid does is cute, but they grow up and [schools] end up expelling them. (Gordon, 1998, p. 426)

A Black teacher at PSA agreed, saying that "if African American and low-income children are coming from authoritarian homes in which discipline is explicit, they will perceive a teacher's lack of explicitness as a weakness" (p. 434). The school's approach to discipline impressed a young White volunteer social worker, who "claimed to be in awe of her colleagues who could work with children that she found incorrigible. She calls it 'firm speaking' and claims that they demand respect and get it" (p. 436). For the researcher,

> the recurring theme throughout these interviews was that, given the racist nature of American society, it is imperative that Black students know what is acceptable behavior. Without strict guidelines that have been reinforced at home and at school, a child might step out of line, open his or her mouth at the wrong time, and face a life of regret for doing so. (p. 436)

At Project Succeed Academy, communication between teachers and students and between teachers and parents was facilitated by the students' case managers. As one researcher explains, PSA students "had to see how their actions were being interpreted by the teachers" and "teachers needed a greater understanding of the lives of their students and what worked in the classroom with 'difficult' children" (Gordon, 1998, p. 424):

> In an attempt to facilitate this dual understanding, the assistant superintendent developed a corps of workers composed of educators, social workers, and paralegal aides to intervene and advocate on behalf of the students. These individuals, called caseworkers, operated in both the schools and the community. Each child was assigned to a caseworker who kept in weekly contact with the child's home, school, and circle of friends and caregivers. (p. 424)

As well as assisting in the development of the contract between students, parents, and the school, case managers were responsible for developing individual academic/social intervention plans; mediating conflicts between students and teachers and between students and other students; observing students in classrooms; recommending appropriate school and/or community services, including attending one of the school's support groups; and keeping in constant contact with parents. Case managers were particularly noted for keeping "the attendance rate high at The Academy" (Henderson-Frye, 1999, p. 105): their first responsibility in the morning was to contact parents of absent students and if necessary to bring unexcused students to the school.

The PSA Program

Project Succeed teachers, staff, and parents worked together to design, develop, and implement a program of total academic, social, and personal immersion for at-risk students (Brown, 2004; Brown & Beckett, in press). In addition to the regular K–8 curriculum followed in all elementary and middle schools in the district, PSA programs included a pullout reading recovery program which provided early intervention for students with literacy problems, after-school homework programs and tutoring sessions staffed by parent and community volunteers, and a Saturday enrichment component, also staffed by parents and community members, which included academic tutoring and field trips to area attractions such as the Cincinnati Zoo, Riverfront Stadium, Wright Patterson Air Force Base, Kentucky Horse Park, and Central State University, a predominantly African American college. Student of the month and honor assemblies recognized students with 3.0 grade point averages and parents who had made significant contributions to the success of the school.

In lieu of physical education, all PSA students were required to take a course in Bushido. Bushido is a form of Judo which teaches the principle of maximum efficiency/minimum effort and the precepts of self-control, patience, flexibility, perseverance, reliability, and respect for others. Eugene Fields, PSA's Bushido instructor, said that though the Bushido "were like knights in old Japan who fought for honor and justice," at Project Succeed,

> the youngsters learn self-discipline, and they learn it is more fun to walk away from a fight than it is to give in to a challenge....A kid comes up to you and says, "I'll kick your butt," and they say, "Maybe tomorrow, but not today" and walk away. I tell all our kids one rule is paramount. If you discipline yourself, nobody else has to do it. Kids pick up on that, but it's not an overnight thing. (Queenan, 1998, p. 1B)

A researcher found that "not all of the students understood Bushido. One informant remarked, 'It shouldn't teach you to fight.'...[But] actual physical restraints are not taught. Rather, children learn an inner sense of well being" (Henderson-Frye, 1999, p. 95) and how "to interact positively with their peers while lessening their fears, aggression and anxieties" (p. 107).

In addition to extra-curricular activities found in many other district schools, including theatre, dance, Suzuki music, and district league baseball and basketball, a hortitherapy program taught students to care for living things, and the school's choir was notable because it included staff and parents as well as students. For the lead author, "the choir was structured as a bonding activity because the parents, the staff and the students perform under the same umbrella that helps to create or accentuate family atmosphere" (Henderson-Frye, 1999, p. 79). The choir performed regularly in concerts, both on campus and in the community.

To immerse students in the PSA environment and to show them that they were welcome and important members of the PSA community, students served on many school committees, as well as on a student court that played an important role in implementing school discipline policies. Most of the students believed that teachers and administrators at their regular schools had punished them unfairly, and this belief was seen by PSA staff to have contributed to the creation of deviant student sub-cultures in regular schools that encouraged disruptive behavior. At PSA, efforts were made to immerse students in a single disciplinary environment where they were supervised and appropriate behavior was required at all times and in all parts of the school and where punishments for infractions were consistently enforced. This was achieved by requiring that all PSA staff from the principal to the cafeteria and custodial workers receive the same training in a range of cooperative discipline and self-discipline techniques and by ensuring that the student court was involved and its decision was heard before any disciplinary action was taken.

The personal needs of individual students at PSA were satisfied through the school's health and wellness program and through the range of support groups the program sponsored. Health and wellness was staffed by volunteer doctors and nurses from the University of Cincinnati, including psychiatric doctors and nurses who dealt with the emotional problems of students and their families. In the health and wellness support groups up to ten students shared with each other family problems such as death, divorce, and drug or alcohol abuse. Students who attended the groups reported looking forward to these sessions. A researcher who shadowed four PSA students two days a week over a period of five weeks concluded that the support groups and the social environment of the school as a whole were having a marked effect on the students' social conduct (Henderson-Frye, 1999). She witnessed behavior which was remarkable given the students involved: students being courteous and polite to each other, students sharing supplies in class, and students bonding with each other, sharing individual accomplishments and personal disappointments and encouraging others to achieve:

> Surprisingly, some students actually demonstrated nurturing tendencies under some circumstances. These tendencies were very apparent in support group sessions where children shared their most personal family experiences that included spousal abuse, substance abuse, child abuse, and abandonment. Members of the group often cried as they related their problems....They were frequently comforted with hugs from their peers...saying "I know how you feel" or "It'll be okay." (p. 100)

Even more remarkable, "such behavior was definitely the rule rather than the exception" (p. 99).

PSA Students

For alternative school students, increased adult presence means more opportunities to develop strong child–adult relationships (Raywid, 1994b, 1995). At Project Succeed, this often meant that students developed a strong relationship with their case manager. For students, case managers were always "there," and many students, given the opportunity to talk with their case manager rather than fight with other students, chose the former. "Beatrice," a well-dressed African American 7th grader who was proud of her accomplishments at the school, was asked how PSA had changed her. She said:

> I had a real attitude last year. I fought a lot....When I first came to The Academy, I had an argument with this girl. The assistant [instructional support person] took me over next door to my case manager. We talked—we talked a lot. She acted like she cared about me. I started talking to her almost every day. I started talking to her when I thought I was going to cream somebody. (Henderson-Frye, 1999, p. 72)

The case manager suggested Beatrice join the health and wellness peer intervention group: "Kids talked about their temper and bad attitudes. We learned how to deal with anger. That's how my case manager says it" (p. 72). When Juanita, a popular, talkative African American 8th grader who had a problem with anger management, was asked how PSA had changed her, she said:

> I'm hostile. I'm easily set off. Somebody just can do a little bitty tiny thing, and it'll set me off to fight....Well, The Academy—I have a case manager....He helped me a lot. I can talk to him about stuff that I can't talk to my mom or my sister about. I have Dr. Green [the acting principal]. There are a lot of people you can talk to instead of just the teachers. (Henderson-Frye, 1999, p. 64)

For other students there were other adults to talk to. In her first week at PSA, India, an attractive, athletic, but also short-tempered African American 6th grader, was taken to see a doctor in the health and wellness room:

> I was mad at him. I didn't feel like being bothered. I guess I said something to him that was wrong. I don't know. He talked to me. After that, I just talk to them all the time....I don't think my temper is as bad [as] it used to be. I can control it more now. I haven't had any big arguments since I have been at this school....I like the school. My parents like it too. They say I've changed, and I don't fly off the handle. (Henderson-Frye, 1999, pp. 74–75)

Increased adult presence at PSA also provided students with the security they needed to live a more normal student life. Kevin, a quiet, well-mannered White 6th grader who was proud of his and his sister's accomplishments at the school, may not at first have seemed an ideal candidate for the Project Succeed program. Though Kevin had had frequent and seemingly unprovoked outbursts at his previous school, he responded well when a PSA doctor recommended an increase in his daily dosage of Ritalin. When interviewed, he was clearly excited about being named PSA student of the week and student of the month: "When I was student of the week, I had a special chair. You saw me. It was that big, soft swivel chair. Remember?" (Henderson-Frye, 1999, p. 70). But Kevin is also described as being quiet and somewhat shy. He is observed opening doors for female teachers. What he seems to value most are his personal relationships, first with his twin sister, but also with his best friend, Ted: "We do a lot together. He says, 'Let's go do this,' so we go and do it. We don't do bad things. If I have a problem, Ted talks to me" (p. 70). When asked whether PSA was an ideal school, Kevin was not sure. Though he didn't think there were any drugs or alcohol—"Dr. Green...wouldn't allow it. The teachers wouldn't" (p. 69)—there were some fights, and in what appears to have been the strongest statement he made during the interview—on a day when he did not take his medication and was more active and talkative—Kevin said that in an ideal school there would be "No fights. There wouldn't be any fights....There wouldn't be any gangs—no gangs" (p. 69).

Conclusion

We began this chapter by asking what an educational environment specifically designed to meet the needs of at-risk students would look like, and we tentatively answered that it would ideally be a separate facility where all students felt they belonged, where teachers were committed to helping their students learn, where parents and community members were actively involved in all aspects of the school's operations, and where district officials were prepared to provide the extra resources that all alternative schools need to succeed. We then looked more closely at Project Succeed Academy, a successful alternative school in Cincinnati which immersed K–8 students in an educational environment which placed equal emphasis on academic, social, and personal development and where the evidence presented overwhelmingly suggests that students felt they belonged and teachers were committed to helping their students. As we will see in Chapter 8, Project Succeed was also a school where parents and community members were actively involved in all aspects of day-to-day operations and where school district officials were prepared to provide the added resources the school needed to support its low student–teacher and student–adult ratios.

Chapter 8

Project Succeed Academy: A School/Family/Community Partnership

Introduction

WE SAW in Chapter 4 that parent involvement in students' school-related activities is associated with improved student behavior and academic achievement but that low-income parents are less involved than middle-class parents and African American parents are involved in different ways than White parents in their children's schooling. Involving parents in student's school-related activities is especially challenging in alternative schools for at-risk students in large urban school districts. Not only do these schools serve mainly low-income and ethnic minority students, but the chronic disruptive behavior in regular schools which led to the students being transferred to alternative schools can often be traced back to a lack of parental involvement at home. The topic of parent involvement is only just beginning to arise in studies of alternative schools for at-risk students, and when it does come up the involvement described is not always positive. In Chapter 1 we cited the example of a grades 4–12 alternative school serving mainly African American students which was established and allowed to continue in existence for 20 years as a form of warehouse for disruptive students before the introduction of drop-out prevention programs and other social services requiring at least some involvement by parents and guardians (Carpenter-Aeby & Aeby, 2001). We also cited the example of group of parents at a public meeting speaking out against a government bill that would have established an alternative school, fearing that the school would label their children and isolate them from mainstream educational opportunities (Dunbar, 1999).

The challenge faced by alternative schools for at-risk students in large urban school districts is to build strong school communities where teachers and parents see themselves as working toward a common goal. To do this, teachers and parents have to overcome cultural differences in the area of student discipline and develop shared norms of behavior they can communicate to students both at school and at home (Gottfredson, 2001). We saw in Chapter 4, however, that the challenges faced by urban schools trying to improve communication between teachers and parents have proved so intractable that researchers in the area of parent involvement have begun to call for fundamental changes in parent–teacher relationships. We cited the example of Smrekar and Cohen-Vogel (2001), who argue that parents should no longer be seen as "supporters, helpers, and fund raisers" but as "decision makers, partners, and collaborators" (p. 87).

In the present study of an alternative school for elementary and middle school students at risk of educational failure in Cincinnati, we show how a new model of parent involvement helped improve communication between predominantly middle-class White teachers and predominantly disadvantaged African American and urban Appalachian parents and how improved communication helped build and sustain a new type of school community. This model of parent involvement represents a twofold extension of the partnership model that is now replacing the support model in some urban schools. First, not only did parents partner with teachers to build a stronger school community, but teachers partnered with parents to build stronger families. Second and perhaps more significant, parents and teachers at the alternative school built and sustained a home–school community which immersed at-risk students, parents, and teachers in a total learning environment (Comer, 1997). The net result, we argue, was that disadvantaged African American and urban Appalachian parents, working together with middle-class White teachers, developed a home–school learning community strong enough to fulfill the original purpose of all schools, namely, to strengthen the larger communities they serve.

Background

In reflecting on his years of service at the school district level and trying to give voice to what he experienced, the lead author of the present volume came to see that the main challenge he faced was to bring parents and teachers together to build consensus on new policies related to student discipline and new approaches to educating at-risk students (Brown, 2004; Brown & Beckett, 2007). Parents and teachers first came together as individuals participating in the Project Succeed summer reading programs, programs that required parental involvement both at home and at school. Engagement continued at the group level when the parents formed a Project Succeed parents association and together with the Cincinnati federation of teachers and other groups and individuals advocated for a year-round Project Succeed Academy housed in its own building and with its own teaching staff. Finally, with board of education approval for an alternative school free to develop new discipline policies and educational programs for the students and families it would serve, the parents association and the school's discipline and curriculum committees, as well as individual parents and teachers, worked together to make Project Succeed Academy a success.

Some of the K–3 students enrolled in the Project Succeed summer programs in 1994 and 1995 had been restless and confrontational, bringing with them to school problems that overwhelmed them at home. Encouraged by the lead author to reach out to the students' families, Project Succeed teachers found that their first task was to work with the students' case managers to connect parents with social service agencies and to advocate on their behalf. Most of the schools' grades 4–8 students, though clearly capable of doing the work Project Succeed required, had developed a resistance to school and a talent for disrupting the work of others. Project Succeed parents wanted their children to take advantage of the opportunities the program provided, but students had come to believe that the same society that disadvantaged their parents was disadvantaging them and they were not listening to their parents. Encouraged by the lead author to become more involved in the Project Succeed program, parents found that their involvement set an example their children began to follow. In facilitating communication between teachers and parents, the lead author began a process that ultimately led to the development of a home–school community in which parents and teachers were equal partners.

The lead author encouraged all parents to become actively involved in PSA because he knew how important it was to create a family atmosphere in the school. The lead author was himself a parent with children in Cincinnati's public schools. He was also a career CPS educator who had worked closely with parents as an elementary art teacher and middle school and high school principal. In the 1980s, parents had helped him turn around the high school he had graduated from 25 years before. The lead author knew that the disruptive behavior of PSA students was the product of school and family factors that only schools and families working together could successfully address. As we saw in Chapter 7, for example, when asked in 1996 to describe some of the programs PSA had implemented to improve the behavior of students he singled out for special mention the school choir. He said that the choir was "structured as a bonding activity" in which students, staff, and parents "perform under the same umbrella" helping to "create or accentuate family atmosphere" (Henderson-Frye, 1999, p. 79).

Project Succeed's Black Parents

By the early 1990s, African American parents in Cincinnati had been engaged with the city's public schools for more than 150 years on issues of segregation and other forms of discrimination. Increasing frustration over the failure of the school district to provide quality education for Black students, especially in the district's seven low-achieving neighborhood schools singled out for special mention in the *Bronson* settlement agreement of 1984, led some disadvantaged Black parents to champion the cause of the successful Project Succeed summer reading program. It was this group of parents which was instrumental in getting the necessary school board approvals and school board and city funding to transform the summer reading program into a year-round school housed in its own building. Like Black communities after the Civil War taking advantage of the support offered by the Freedmen's Bureau and the Northern philanthropic societies or the Black community in Cincinnati in the 1850s taking advantage of the city's decision to fund a separate Black system on the same basis as it funded its White school system, Project Succeed was a community-wide effort that capitalized on an unusual demonstration of school board, city, and private support to promote what was essentially a community school. For the parents involved, Project Succeed would be their school and for them, given the state of their neighborhood schools, the label "alternative" would have only positive connotations.

It was also these parents who took the lead in the Project Succeed parents association and organized the continuing involvement of parents in all aspects of the school's operation. Two features of Project Succeed which made the school a real alternative to Black neighborhood schools, features also found in Black schools during Reconstruction and throughout segregation, were the extent and quality of home–school communications and the extent and continuity of student supervision provided within the context of a single home–school community. We saw in Chapter 5 that during Reconstruction and throughout segregation, after playing a key role in establishing a school, in soliciting and providing financial support beyond what was provided by government, and in hiring a principal, Black parents gave the principal and the teachers he hired considerable freedom to develop and implement a curriculum in line with their educational philosophy (Siddle Walker, 2003). But if Black parents in the past were less able to partner with teachers in pedagogical matters, we also saw that teachers and parents worked closely together in the area of student discipline, with parents frequently being called to the school and teachers frequently calling at parents' homes after school (Dempsey & Noblit, 1993a, b).

Though class differences were apparent during segregation and in the early years of desegregation became a major concern in some all-Black schools (Gouldner, 1978; Rist, 1973/2002), the dominant theme in the history of separate Black education is a shared sense of community during a period when the advancement of the race took precedence over the advancement of individuals. This sense of community was best expressed in the partnerships formed between schools and families to immerse children in a single, coherent, consistent, and continuous disciplinary environment. One is reminded of Charleston-born, college-educated Mamie Garvin Fields teaching in poor, isolated James Island, South Carolina, in the early years of the last century. As mentioned in Chapter 5, her pedagogy teachers had told her "at all times to keep close to the parents" (Garvin Fields, 1983, p. 99), and on James Island she found that an effective way of disciplining students who misbehaved was to threaten to bring their parents up to the school: "since the children didn't like that, they behaved" (p. 99).

At Project Succeed, the quality of home–school communications was especially high (Brown, 2004). First, bi-weekly conferences sustained individual parent–teacher partnerships on academic matters, with parents being expected to follow up on the conferences and offer their children enrichment activities at home. Second, the parents association sustained numerous parent–school partnerships on academic matters by recruiting parent volunteers to offer enrichment activities in the school library after school and on Saturdays. Third and most important, parent–teacher partnerships on discipline matters were facilitated by case managers who observed student–teacher interactions and conferenced with teachers in their classrooms, observed student–parent interactions and talked with parents about discipline concerns during home visits, and attended parent–teacher meetings designed to get to the root of students' problem behaviors and to find ways to correct them.

Equally important, the Project Succeed program, in implementing its philosophy of immersing students in a total educational environment and recognizing the importance of students at risk of educational failure developing personally and socially as well as academically, emphasized continuous and extensive adult supervision of all student activities (Brown, 2004). With the support of the many parents and community members who came to the school daily, Project Succeed Academy was able to organize a range of supervised activities for students before and after school, at noon and in the evening, and on Saturdays and during the summer. The support of parents and community members also ensured that students received supervision when they were not participating in organized activities. Parents and community members volunteered to supervise students on the school buses and playgrounds, in the hallways, lunchroom, and gym, and even in the bathrooms (Henderson-Frye, 1999).

Project Succeed's White Parents

In the 1990s, Cincinnati's Appalachian communities were generally newer and less politically active than the city's African American communities. Furthermore, Appalachian parents were less involved in their children's school-related activities than Black parents, even though Appalachian students' levels of academic achievement and drop-out rates were generally worse than those of Black students. The drop-out rate among Appalachian students in Cincinnati, for example, was worse than the rates found in the Appalachian counties of eastern Kentucky (Obermiller, Borman, & Kroger, 1988). Seeing their children progress in the Project Succeed summer programs, however, and encouraged by the PSA parents association, many Appalachian parents became actively involved in the year-round academy. Without the levels of support offered by relatives and neighbors in older, better-established working-class communities and which were characteristic of the rural Appalachian counties from which they or their parents had migrated, urban Appalachian parents in Cincinnati, many of whom were single mothers, came to rely on Project Succeed as a form of alternative community for themselves as well as for their children.

Before becoming involved, however, urban Appalachian parents had to overcome the feeling that Project Succeed was not their school. In a study of Appalachian youth attending a summer job skills program in Lower Price Hill at this time, researchers found that most of the youth felt alienated from their predominantly Black high school (Penn, Borman, & Hoeweler, 1994). As one student said, "[Y]ou don't feel right when it's a black culture month, black this and that....It's all about blacks, and you feel out of place" (p. 127). For Jerry, an experienced Appalachian teacher in Cincinnati, "what it really boils down to is...economics—coming from the same neighborhood where blacks and whites share a low class economy. At the school the black student is given more prestige than the white student" (p. 129). Outside of school, however, things were different: the researchers found, for example, that "Lower Price Hill gangs include both black and white members. According to one white youth, a particular black member 'motivates [the other members]....He's a tough kid'" (p. 134). The difference between Project Succeed and the students' regular schools was that as a district-wide alternative school, it adopted admission policies which ensured that school demographics matched district demographics as a whole and a philosophy of inclusiveness was systematically communicated from teachers to students, from the director to the parents association, and from the parents association to all parents. As we indicated in Chapter 7, this effort was successful and one of the teachers-in-charge was able to report that Project Succeed Academy did not have any serious racial problems in its first full year of operation (Henderson-Frye, 1999).

We saw in Chapter 2 that working-class parents are generally less involved in their children's school-related activities than middle-class parents (Moles, 1993) and that lower levels of involvement by working-class parents have been linked to lower educational aspirations for their children (Lareau, 1987, 2000). The research suggests that so long as their children are getting along well enough academically and socially, many working-class parents feel comfortable leaving their children's education in the hands of teachers. For Project Succeed parents, however, this sort of complacency was not an option: by the time their children enrolled in Project Succeed they knew that their children were in serious trouble, and with the program itself requiring extensive involvement there seemed to be no choice but to partner with the school to find a solution. Recruited by and working with other parents whose children were having difficulties and kept in constant communication with teachers directly through required bi-weekly conferences and indirectly through students' case managers, Appalachian parents in Cincinnati who before had had limited and largely negative contact with their children's schools now found a way to be more positively involved.

We have also seen that many working-class parents find it difficult to engage with their children's schools on the issue of student discipline, often feeling that schools unfairly punish their children when they try to defend themselves (Lareau, 1996). We also note that in an early study of the Lower Price Hill community in Cincinnati researchers found that "persistent Appalachian values of independence and individuality" resulted in children growing up in homes where "conformity in terms of obedience to authority is not prized" (Borman, Lippincott, & Matey, 1978, p. 73). Though in the kindergarten class that was the subject of this study the "children's values appear to have influenced their teacher's behavior" and "child-referenced rather than authority-involving appeals are more likely to be used by the teacher to gain an appropriate response from children" (p. 84), the same could not be said of other classrooms in the school or of classrooms in other schools attended by urban Appalachian students at this time. At Project Succeed, on the other hand, operating under a new district-wide code of behavior of which the school itself was an important part, all students were given the opportunity to resolve conflicts with other students by talking through them with their case managers, the code itself explicitly recognized self-defense as a legitimate justification for fighting (Barton, Coley, & Wenglinsky, 1998), and the school's student court had a formal role in the discipline process (Brown, 2004). All of these factors ensured that no disciplinary action was taken except in serious cases of misconduct and only after student and family perspectives were taken into account.

Teachers Partnering with Parents

Project Succeed developed an educational philosophy under which the school enrolled families as well as students (Brown, 2004). While the focus of the PSA student/parent/school contracts was on the students and what they were required to do to succeed, the contracts also specified what parents were required to do to support students and what PSA staff were required to do to support parents. PSA staff compiled daily reports that kept parents up to date on their children's progress. Parents were required to read, sign, and return the reports to the school the next day. Parents were also expected to use the reports to guide them in providing enrichment activities at home, and PSA staff provided parents with the support they needed to do this effectively. All parents were required to attend bi-weekly conferences. These conferences included instruction from PSA teachers on how to help their children at home. The instruction was given in make-and-take activities rather than lectures or presentations. PSA teachers modeled observation and questioning techniques parents could use to extend students' thinking at home, and parents had the opportunity to practice under the guidance of experts. In some cases, PSA contracts also included steps the parents had to take to improve their academic skills, and PSA teachers provided counseling services to help guide them. Some parents, after consulting with PSA teachers, enrolled in high school completion programs and obtained general equivalency degrees. PSA staff also organized voluntary Saturday sessions where parents were introduced to "crucial developmental issues such as the possible causes, effects, and preventative measures to be taken with attention deficit disorder" (Gordon, 1998, p. 424). According to an observer at the time, "it is not unusual to have 50 parents show up on a Saturday with their children" (p. 424).

PSA contracts required the school to support parents in more practical ways. PSA case managers, for example, provided transportation for parents to attend meetings at the school, helped some parents enter drug and alcohol treatment programs, and represented other parents in negotiations with social service agencies and with the juvenile justice system. Case managers also helped parents with such basic needs as housing, heat and light, legal issues, and medical attention. If parents had problems paying their bills or had to make court appearances, for example, case managers went with them to help resolve the problems. But PSA was not just a social service program for needy families. Case managers may have helped parents satisfy their immediate needs and teachers may have helped improve their academic skills, but PSA parents also responded by becoming more actively and more positively involved in the day-to-day activities of the school.

Parents Partnering with Teachers

We have already mentioned that the Project Succeed parents association was instrumental in getting the necessary school board approvals and school board and city funding to transform the summer reading program into a year-round school housed in its own building. The lead author had encouraged the parents association to become active in gaining additional financial support the full-year school would need (Brown, 2004; Brown & Beckett, 2007). Parent testimonials were crucial in obtaining substantial grants from Cincinnati City Council and the University of Cincinnati and smaller grants and numerous in-kind contributions from city-wide and local community businesses, organizations, and individuals. The lead author also lobbied the Cincinnati board of education to hold a public forum on the full-year proposal. So many parents volunteered to speak in support of Project Succeed that the venue for the forum had to be changed three times. In the end, more than 400 parents and 100 community members turned out to argue from personal experience that a year-round school based on the Project Succeed model was needed. Equally important, the parents witnessed a majority-White school board demonstrating a rare commitment to minority education by instructing staff to accommodate all parents and community members who wished to speak at the forum, listening to as many testimonials as time permitted, and approving the full-year proposal and providing most of the funding needed to support it.

We have also said that the Project Succeed parents association took the lead in recruiting parent and community volunteers and involving them in all aspects of the year-round school operations. As a result of their efforts, parents sat on school committees, volunteered in classrooms and tutorial sessions and on field trips, organized fundraising events, and continued to reach out to individuals and groups in the local community to solicit in-kind services and other contributions. Parents succeeded in recruiting an account executive from the city's largest public relations firm to lead the school's communication effort; lawyers, accountants, and other professionals who offered pro bono hours to help with a range of school, school board, and city council issues relating to opening a new year-round school; many local businesses and individuals who donated resources and thousands of dollars' worth of in-kind contributions; and government, religious, sports, and business leaders with connections to the community who served as tutors, mentors, and motivational speakers.

The parents association published a monthly newsletter describing parent activities and recruiting parents for upcoming activities. It also organized evening events, Saturday picnics, and field trips specifically for parents. These parent gatherings always ended with the school song. Under the leadership of the parents association, Project Succeed became the focal point for a new, stronger local community, a community which provided additional support for individual parents. The importance of parental involvement at Project Succeed was recognized by school staff. When surveyed as part of an evaluation, the program staff expressed strongest agreement on the importance of family involvement and on communication with parents through the use of the daily progress reports, weekly meetings, and phone calls (Brown, 2004). The importance of parent involvement was also formally recognized by the school, with parents being honored along with students at noon assemblies for their contributions to the school.

Parents and Teachers Working Together

As parents became more involved in Project Succeed, the lead author helped them understand that the message students were bringing to the school from home was not the message most parents intended: however alienated parents might feel from the larger society, they also wanted their children to seize the opportunity the school provided to work toward a more promising future for themselves and their own children. Similarly, working with PSA teachers, the lead author helped them see that beneath the veneer of failure, disengagement, and disruption lay a deeper desire in students to succeed for themselves and for their families. The most important lesson Project Succeed students learned at the school came from seeing their parents and teachers working together in a spirit of cooperation and with a common purpose. When PSA parents became actively involved in the school and when PSA teachers acted as if they expected students to succeed, students began to see themselves less at risk and more at promise (Swadener & Lubeck, 1995).

In their regular schools PSA students had felt excluded and they acted accordingly. At Project Succeed, teachers, parents, and community members came together to create a school where students felt welcomed and encouraged and where their behavior and academic achievement improved dramatically. Parents were in PSA classrooms helping teachers create learning environments in which students experienced academic success, many for the first time. Parents were in the hallways, lunchroom, gym, and playing field, helping create social environments in which clear rules and strict rule enforcement ensured student safety and security and made it less likely that students would, as one put it, "fly off the handle." But perhaps the most significant contribution parents made to the success of Project Succeed was their ability to reach out to and connect the school with the larger community. It was not just that the school was there for students: through its connections with the business community, universities and hospitals, professional sports teams, and much more, it seemed as if the city of Cincinnati was there for them too. Students soon realized, as their parents had done, that PSA was theirs if they wanted it, and most students took the school up on its offer.

Conclusion

The lead author believed that schools should assume more responsibility for facilitating and coordinating the educational efforts of adults and provide more opportunities for parents and community members to learn from teachers and for teachers to learn from parents and community members. As we have seen in this chapter, at Project Succeed Academy encouraging parents' and other family members' participation in the education of students was a primary focus at all grade levels: daily progress reports, bi-weekly conferences, and regular parent night meetings established communications between teachers and parents; teachers showing parents how they could help their children at home and parents becoming involved in all aspects of the school's operation established a true partnership between them.

Without the involvement of parents, Project Succeed Academy could not have succeeded in its aim of immersing students in a holistic learning environment. With their participation at the school, the Project Succeed program offered an enriched classroom learning environment that was extended beyond the classroom to include supervision and instruction in the hallways, lunchroom, library, gym, and playground. For Project Succeed students, the school was anywhere and everywhere. Just as important, because parent participation was unusually high, especially for an alternative school for at-risk students, with parent volunteers staffing after-school, evening, Saturday, and summer programs and tutoring their own children at home, it could also be said that Project Succeed was anytime and every time. Looking back now, with the wisdom of hindsight, the lead author can see that PSA students' behavior and academic achievement improved because parents and teachers gave them no other option.

Chapter 9

White Teachers and Black Preachers: An Alliance Made in Heaven?

Introduction

WHEN Project Succeed Academy opened its doors for the first time in August 1995, the school represented the culmination of a four-year effort by the Cincinnati Public Schools office of student discipline to develop and implement new policies and programs designed to respond to what was perceived to be a crisis in student discipline. As already mentioned, Project Succeed was developed in conjunction with a new district-wide code of student behavior. Under the code, elementary and middle school principals had the option of recommending that chronically disruptive students enroll in Project Succeed for up to six months in lieu of suspension. The code of behavior was the result of the district's first comprehensive review of disciplinary policies and programs at all CPS schools and its first attempt to develop a coherent and consistent set of district-wide policies based on research into best practices in the area of student discipline. The code's development required substantive agreement among all major stakeholder groups, including groups with different perspectives on the issue of student discipline generally and a recent history of mistrust and conflict over the issue of student suspensions and expulsions.

We saw in Chapter 7 that in the early 1990s a new superintendent's get-tough approach to discipline had resulted in student suspensions soaring from 11,686 in 1990–1991 to 20,594 in 1991–1992. In addition, new state regulations now allowed Ohio schools to expel students for up to 80 days at a time. The new approach to disruptive students had been demanded by the Cincinnati federation of teachers as part of on-going contract negotiations. The federation in turn was responding to the demands of its members, who were saying that student disruption had become endemic since the Cincinnati school board banned corporal punishment in 1988. The new superintendent's approach to student discipline had also exacerbated long-standing disparities in the suspension and expulsion rates of Black and White students at a time when the district was under pressure from the city's Black community to satisfy the terms of a 1984 school desegregation agreement that required it to adopt race-neutral discipline practices. The Baptist Minister's Conference of Cincinnati and Vicinity, the city's most visible and influential group of African American ministers, had taken the lead in championing the cause of Black families in the district who believed that school discipline policies and procedures unfairly targeted their children.

Project Succeed Academy was designed for the small minority of district students who were most at risk of educational failure in their regular schools. As we saw in Chapter 8, it provided students with an alternative educational environment which addressed their academic, social, and personal needs. But the Project Succeed program also reached out to regular schools with large numbers of at-risk students by establishing centers in the schools where students could be referred in lieu of suspension and centers in the community where students could be referred after they were suspended (Brown, 2004). It was in this way that many of the specific disciplinary policies and practices associated with the Project Succeed program came to be adopted by many of the district's regular schools. Furthermore, as we will see in this chapter, when supporters of the Project Succeed program, including the teachers federation and the ministers conference, reached out to the district and the school board, the general approach to discipline in the alternative program was adopted as the basis of the new district-wide code of student behavior. It was through the district-wide code of student behavior that the Project Succeed approach to addressing the needs of at-risk students penetrated the district as a whole. Project Succeed policies and programs continue today, then, in many district schools and in the district-wide code of behavior, even though Project Succeed Academy has been closed.

A Discipline Advisory Board

In reflecting on his work in the area of student discipline throughout the 1990s, the lead author came to see that his role as facilitator of communication and mediator of conflict across socioeconomic and ethnic lines, however important it was in his work with Project Succeed, was crucial in his larger effort to develop and implement a comprehensive set of new discipline policies and programs that would help resolve the district's crisis in student discipline. With Project Succeed the lead author could continue in the role he had adopted as a school leader in the 1980s, namely, that of chief advocate for disadvantaged students and families whose needs were not being addressed by the larger community. As in the role played by Black principals during segregation and as in the role he had played as principal at Bloom and Withrow, the lead author either spoke out for silenced communities or created contexts, such as the school board forum described in Chapter 8, in which parents and community members could speak for themselves. With the new district-wide code of behavior, however, the lead author's role was different. Rather than advocate for particular policies and programs, even for the policies and programs being developed as part of the early Project Succeed summer programs, his main role was to involve all stakeholder groups in a development process that would result in substantive agreement on and commitment to a new set of disciplinary policies and programs among groups holding very different views and with a recent history of mistrust and opposition.

The Cincinnati Public Schools office of student discipline was created by the board of education in 1991 to address the problem of soaring student suspension and expulsion rates in the district. The first step the lead author took on assuming the directorship of the office was to form a discipline advisory board (Brown & Beckett, 2006). The discipline advisory board was a broad-based coalition of concerned individuals that included representatives from the Cincinnati federation of teachers, the Baptist ministers conference, and the school administrators association, as well as representatives and individuals from the business community, local universities, the health care professions, mental health agencies, community activist groups, and parent groups. Advisory board members were told at the beginning of their work that they were entering into a process which required consensual decision making, and they agreed that to reach consensus they would have to explore territory beyond their obvious differences. Board members were also told that for the development process to be successful they would have to advocate on behalf of the new policies and programs they agreed to with the groups they represented, and they agreed that effective advocacy would require a degree of commitment beyond surface acquiescence.

The composition of the discipline advisory board reflected the lead author's two main concerns in developing Cincinnati's first district-wide code of student behavior. First, he was concerned that teachers and administrators in the district hear from important stakeholder groups outside the district. Representatives from the universities, for example, included experts on best practices in the area of student discipline who could introduce Cincinnati teachers and administrators to new research-based policies and programs that were proving to be successful in reducing suspension and expulsion rates in other urban school systems. Health care professionals could tell teachers and administrators about some of the physical and mental challenges at-risk students faced, including the challenges faced by large numbers of children being diagnosed with attention deficit disorder. Finally, representatives from the Cincinnati business community, which had a long history of involvement in the city's public schools (Borman & Spring, 1984) and which included several large corporations competing nationally and internationally, could speak about the effect the crisis in student discipline was having on the city's image and on the resulting difficulties they were having attracting top people to Cincinnati.

Second, the lead author was concerned that teachers and school administrators hear from important stakeholder groups within the district on the issues of soaring suspension and expulsion rates and of increasing racial imbalance in student discipline. Representatives from the city's Black community, including members of parent and activist groups as well as the Baptist ministers conference, could tell teachers and administrators about disciplinary practices common in students' homes and communities and about the challenges students faced when students were confronted with conflicting disciplinary practices in their schools. The main challenge the discipline advisory board faced was to overcome differences between the federation of teachers, which took a legal approach to discipline and which, as we have seen, would adopt a formal policy of zero tolerance of student misconduct in 1993, and the Baptist ministers conference, which advocated an instructional approach to discipline in schools and which would successfully campaign against a proposed school tax levy to protest the district's high rates of suspension and expulsion among African American students, also in 1993. As other advisory board members were similarly divided over the general approach they believed the district should take to student misbehavior, no solution to the crisis in student discipline in Cincinnati's public schools would be possible unless the discipline advisory board took full account of both legal and instructional approaches.

The mandate of the discipline advisory board was to examine the full range of approaches to student discipline and to advise the board of education on their appropriateness. The board surveyed staff, teachers, and parents within the district to determine prevailing opinions on student discipline in general and on the need for a new district-wide code of behavior in particular. The board also reviewed the research literature on best practices in the area of student discipline and examined other school districts' policies and programs, especially those urban districts that dealt with large numbers of chronically disruptive students. The board found that different groups had significantly different views that could be resolved only if the district adopted a collaborative approach to the problem of student discipline. The board believed that gaining support for a new district-wide code of behavior would require the development of a strong consensus among the various voices in the district and in the wider community and it recommended that the development process include focus group research, guided mediation, and an agreement from all factions to accept the new code of behavior in a collaborative manner. Among their specific recommendations, the discipline advisory board advocated following up on Junious Williams' finding that the district was less responsive to the needs of its Black students with a new look at the issue of fighting. Rather than students facing automatic suspension, the board suggested that they might be sent to a "time out room to address what happened, why, and develop an action plan identifying more appropriate behaviors for the future" ("Discipline in city schools," 1993).

As a result of the discipline advisory board's initial findings, the lead author formed several teams to address the conflicts among groups on various issues, including a team to develop the concept of an alternative school for at-risk students. He recruited representatives from the different stakeholder groups—principals, teachers, parents, businesspeople, union officials, ministers, doctors and health care workers, attorneys, government officials, and university faculty—and ensured that each team included a broad range of interests and opinions. The team formed to develop the alternative school concept was particularly diverse, including a high school drop-out and a doctor of philosophy, a welfare recipient and a millionaire, a manual laborer and a medical doctor, a corporate executive and the head of a government agency, a church conference chair and a community activist, as well as school administrators, teachers, and parents. The lead author made it clear in facilitating these teams that on the issue of student discipline the voices of all participants counted. He said that disagreement was welcome, so long as team members agreed to work through their differences toward a consensus on recommendations to improve discipline. Remarkably, most team members quickly developed a sense of shared authority and shared responsibility. Tension and conflict, apparent in the teams' first meetings, were replaced by a sense of common purpose and a spirit of cohesiveness.

An Intervention

As an African American educator with more than 20 years experience as a teacher and administrator in Cincinnati's racially divided public schools, the lead author knew firsthand how important critical race theory's notion of interest convergence could be. Advancing the cause of disadvantaged minority students had always involved a combination of steady hard work with the students and their families, largely out of sight and mind of the larger community, and seizing the moment when the larger community turned its attention to at-risk students and making the most of the limited resources that were briefly made available. Now was clearly a time when the interests of disadvantaged minority students and their families were converging with the interests of the larger community, and the lead author felt he could put pressure on the ministers conference, activist groups, and parents to seize the moment and come to an agreement with the school district on issues relating to student discipline. At the same time, the teachers federation was under pressure to resolve the issue as well: business leaders were saying that the crisis was hurting the city, health care professionals were saying that the problems many students faced could not be resolved simply by taking a legal approach to disruptive behavior, and university researchers were saying that new instructional approaches to discipline were proving successful in other urban school districts.

It was at this point in the development process that the lead author requested a meeting with the executive councils of the ministers conference and the teachers federation with the intention of mediating the differences between the two groups. As a result of this meeting, the ministers and teachers agreed to work more in harmony with each other (Clark, 1993). The value of this cooperation became clear in the final stages of the process, when the two groups formed an alliance and together advocated on behalf of Project Succeed Academy and the district-wide code of behavior before the board of education (Clark, 1995). It was at this meeting that the federation of teachers and the Baptist ministers conference, after receiving input from their representatives on the discipline advisory board, recognized that beyond their superficial differences lay an area of substantial agreement and that the advisory board had found a viable way to resolve the differences that remained. The basis of this agreement was, first, recognition on the part of the ministers that, apart from the specific issue of racial imbalance in the administration of discipline, zero tolerance for misconduct was consistent with disciplinary practices found in most students' homes and communities and, second, recognition on the part of the teachers that, separate from the issue of pervasive disruption and threats of violence in schools, zero tolerance for misconduct should not be equated with automatic suspension or expulsion and that there was a need for district schools to implement a range of pre-suspension policies and programs specifically designed to meet the needs of at-risk students.

For the lead author, the notion of interest convergence seems necessary to explain what brought these groups together and the general outcomes of their work. Clearly it was in the interest of teachers and administrators in regular schools to have their most disruptive students enrolled in an alternative school, and just as clearly it was in the interests of those advocating on behalf of disadvantaged minority students to have in place in regular schools pre-suspension programs specifically designed to meet their needs. But the lead author also feels that interest convergence is not sufficient to account for what actually occurred in the development process and for how the process was experienced by key participants. What was remarkable to him and to them was how much more energy and creativity went into the process after it became clear that self-interest would be satisfied. Once it was acknowledged by all parties that each group had a legitimate concern, that each group's concern could be satisfied without sacrificing the legitimate concerns of other groups, and that research on best practices in student discipline showed them a viable way forward, a sense of common purpose took hold and members re-doubled their efforts to develop specific policies and programs to meet the needs of at-risk students.

Resolving Conflict over Conflict Resolution

Many of the substantive differences between members of the discipline advisory board were clarified in discussions relating to a program of conflict resolution (Brown & Beckett, 2007). A social service agency, with the support of some community groups, had convinced the board of education to pilot conflict resolution, a set of mediating principles that were intended to help students negotiate conflict to zero. These were proven strategies in middle-class White schools where parents taught the same principles to their children at home. For many disadvantaged Black students, however, the strategies conflicted with what they were being taught at home, where the basic message from parents was, When you're struck, strike back—or I'll strike you. The net result was that in most Cincinnati schools student suspensions as a result of fighting continued at the same high levels as before the introduction of conflict resolution and the program's principles were assessed as ineffectual by district staff.

For the lead author, the essence of the situation was that the district was paying a lot of money for a program that was not working, and this money was needed to support programs, such as Project Succeed, which were working. At a regular school board meeting where it would be decided whether conflict resolution should be adopted on a permanent basis, the lead author presented data from an early assessment of the Project Succeed summer program to show the program's superior potential for improving student discipline in the district (Brown, 2004). The lead author also arranged for Project Succeed parents to speak at the meeting, and board members later told him informally that it was the parents' input which decided the issue. The parents spoke about Project Succeed's health and wellness programs, its Bushido martial arts instruction, and especially its Star Curriculum of violence prevention and conflict resolution through role-playing and decision-making training. The parents' testimonials convinced the board to leave discipline program choices up to individual schools and to re-allocate conflict resolution funds to the office of student discipline. These decisions allowed the lead author to promote the success of Project Succeed programs to district schools with large numbers of at-risk students and to provide the schools with financial support for alternative learning centers based on the Project Succeed model. At the same time, conflict resolution was adopted as a program the office of student discipline would support, and when discipline committees at other district schools requested resources for implementing the program the office of student discipline provided them. The net result was that individual schools were now in a better position to implement discipline programs they believed would be most effective with their student populations, and schools with large numbers of at-risk students had for the first time access to programs that were proven to be successful in other urban school districts with similar student populations.

A District-wide Code of Behavior

Cincinnati's district-wide code of student behavior addressed the need for consistent discipline policies across the district by listing student behaviors leading to suspension and behaviors leading to mandatory suspension with recommendation for expulsion (Barton, Coley, & Wenglinsky, 1998). The code also addressed the need for flexibility within the district by listing options from which local school discipline committees could choose in developing pre-suspension programs designed to encourage students to learn self-discipline. As we have seen, the discipline advisory board had taken a collaborative approach in developing Cincinnati's new district-wide code of behavior. Now the code itself emphasized the importance of all stakeholders taking a collaborative approach to maintaining discipline. The overall purpose of the code was to protect the rights and define the responsibilities of everyone involved with the city's public schools. According to the code, students, teachers, staff members, administrators, and parents had the right to a safe and orderly environment in which their children could learn and work and to which they could entrust them. But to protect these rights, students, teachers, staff members, administrators, and parents also had specific responsibilities they had to fulfill. According to the code:

- Students are expected to attend school, to prepare for school, to participate in classes and activities, and to prevent and resolve problems.
- Teachers are expected to prepare, to create positive learning environments, to evaluate student performance in informal and formal ways, and to communicate with parents, staff, and administrators.
- Staff members are expected to contribute to creating a positive learning environment, to provide guidance and support, to provide supplementary resources and materials, and to provide a nutritious daily lunch.
- Administrators are expected to work in collaboration with faculty and other staff to create a positive learning environment and to provide instructional leadership.
- Parents are expected to set high expectations for their children, to communicate with their children, to help their children learn, to encourage and praise their children, and to monitor their children's education.

After gaining school board approval for the new district-wide code of behavior, the office of student discipline took several important steps to support local schools in implementing the code and to help facilitate development of the consensus that was essential if the code of behavior was to be effective (Brown & Beckett, 2006). First, the code was distributed in two handbooks, written in age- and developmentally appropriate language, for students in grades K–6 and 7–12, and a videotape was prepared to introduce the code to students, teachers, and other stakeholders. Second, all teachers in the district were provided with an instructional manual designed to help them develop lessons plans to teach the code to students. Third, standardized discipline referral forms were developed for all schools, with different forms to be used for grades K–6 and grades 7–12. Fourth, school discipline committees were required to implement the code in a way that reflected the beliefs and practices of their local school communities. Schools were encouraged to follow the example of the office of student discipline in involving all stakeholders in the development of their plans and in seeking consensus among stakeholders before implementing their plans' individual components. Finally, school discipline committees were specifically asked to develop age- and developmentally appropriate alternatives to suspension for serious offences such as fighting.

To address the issue of high rates of suspension and expulsion in most Cincinnati schools, the district-wide code of behavior included a new category of offenses and consequences. In addition to student behaviors leading to suspension and to mandatory suspension with recommendation for expulsion, the code included a category of behaviors leading to enrollment in pre-suspension programs. Working with local school discipline committees to implement the code, the lead author emphasized the importance of developing pre-suspension programs that would be effective with their student populations. Among the innovative pre-suspension options developed by local school discipline committees and supported by the office of student discipline were tough love groups—students could be required to attend a number of meetings equal to the number of days they would have been suspended; behavioral contracts—students could be required to develop with teachers and parents a behavioral contract detailing specific outcomes for specific behaviors; and student/parent in-school suspension—students could be required to be in separate in-school suspension with a parent. These pre-suspension programs proved to be effective in reducing student suspension and expulsion because they functioned as a sort of time-out for both students and teachers ("Discipline in city schools," 1993) and because the time made available was used for either intensive behavioral support or for students, teachers, and parents to work together to reach consensus on what amounted to individual codes of behavior.

To address the issue of disparities in the suspension and expulsion of Black and White students, Cincinnati's district-wide code of behavior required all district schools to apply the same standards of discipline and to follow the same disciplinary procedures. The code defined disciplinary offenses, prescribed specific consequences for specific disruptive behaviors, and laid out a clear path of increasing consequences for increasingly disruptive behaviors. On the issue of fighting, the code explicitly recognized self-defense as a legitimate justification for fighting. At the same time, the code encouraged local school discipline committees to develop violence prevention programs appropriate for their school communities.

A Need for External Funding

Still unresolved in the development process was the issue of external funding for discipline initiatives supported by the office of student discipline which could not be funded from the resources made available by the school board. The issue was especially acute in the case of the year-round, stand-alone Project Succeed Academy and the alternative learning centers inspired by the Project Succeed program which were proposed for regular schools with large numbers of at-risk students. An incident occurred in the spring of 1995 which gave the lead author an opportunity to facilitate communication more broadly between the city's disadvantaged African American communities and its middle-class White communities. On April 25, a police officer was monitoring a group of high school–age youths who had gathered during school hours on a street in Cincinnati's downtown shopping and business area. When asked by the officer to leave, the young people refused, and when one young man was told he was under arrest for disorderly conduct, he resisted being handcuffed. The incident quickly escalated: the police officer applied a chemical irritant to subdue the young man, the young man's friends appeared ready to intervene, more police officers arrived on the scene, and violence broke out between the youths and the police.

A videotape of this incident was shown on local television news programs that evening. The next day Cincinnati's city manager requested an investigation into the circumstances surrounding the incident ("Beating by police angers Cincinnatians," 1995). Some of the young people involved in the incident were students in Cincinnati's public schools. The next day and for several weeks after the incident, the lead author and office of student discipline case managers swept the streets of the downtown area encouraging young people not to obstruct doorways to businesses and to be courteous to citizens. Their daily presence was noted and gratefully appreciated by members of the downtown business community. Recognizing another area in which the interests of Cincinnati's Black and White communities were converging, the lead author seized the opportunity presented by the incident to initiate a dialogue with representatives from business groups on the initiatives the office of student discipline was taking and on how the business community might become more involved.

Over the next year, more downtown businesspeople joined the discipline advisory board and the teams formed to develop the board's various initiatives. They also solicited material and financial resources in support of the Project Succeed program from various groups and organizations and were able to guarantee most of the external funding the school board needed before it could approve the year-round school and the alternative learning centers (Brown, 2004). The lead author, in facilitating the involvement of the downtown business community, was bringing predominantly White businesspeople into extended and purposeful contact with disadvantaged Black parents, some for the first time. They learned that beneath the truancy and hooliganism they had witnessed on downtown streets there was the belief of Black students and parents that they were being denied their rightful place in the city's public schools. Black parents learned that behind the racism and classism they had long perceived in downtown businesspeople there was a genuine concern that too little was being done to bridge the gaps between the city's two oldest ethnic communities. Like Northern philanthropists in the 19th century, they were only waiting for the Black community to take the initiative and suggest ways they could help. The disciplinary advisory board and its need for external support provided a context and an opportunity to work together to resolve issues affecting both communities and to initiate reforms in the city's public schools that would help create environments where disadvantaged minority students felt they belonged.

Conclusion

The Cincinnati Public Schools district-wide code of behavior remains in effect to this day. As mentioned in Chapter 7, the code has been modified over the years to reflect changes in the structure of K–8 schools in the district, to respond better to an increase in gang violence since the plan's inception, and to respond to changes in state and federal laws. For the lead author, the code's longevity is testament to a development and review process that involved all stakeholders in the district and the wider community and which required stakeholders to work through their superficial differences to find common ground on the substantive issues facing them. The code's longevity is also a testament to the flexibility of the overall approach stakeholders agreed to adopt for reducing suspensions through multiple pre-suspension options developed by local school discipline committees. By incorporating the strengths of both instructional and legal approaches to student discipline and at the same time minimizing the effect each approach might have when adopted in isolation and by encouraging local discipline committees to follow a similar development process to the one followed at the district level and to reach out to all stakeholders in their school communities, Cincinnati's district-wide code of student behavior has helped schools with large numbers of at-risk students create school disciplinary environments in which disadvantaged minority students feel they are treated more fairly and teachers feel safer and more focused on instruction without adversely affecting the efforts of other schools with different student populations to deal with different sets of disciplinary issues.

Chapter 10

Conclusion

PUBLIC SCHOOL districts began experimenting with alternative forms of schooling for students at risk of educational failure in the late 1960s. Since then, according to Raywid (1995), school districts have been relying on their alternative schools for "many of the most promising proposals for improving the education of at-risk students—as well as many of the most popular reform recommendations for the education of all students" (p. 119). It was not until the early 1980s that public school districts began experimenting with remedial schools for at-risk elementary and middle school students. Remedial schools were intended to stimulate academic, social, and personal growth by providing small and supportive learning environments with "positive student-adult relationships, and considerable amounts of individual attention" (p. 128). Unlike other alternative programs, however, remedial schools were also expected to return students to regular schools prepared to succeed in their larger and less-supportive learning environments, and when students' disruptive behavior and academic underachievement returned to pre–alternative school levels, remedial schools were perceived to have been educational experiments that had failed (Carpenter-Aeby & Aeby, 2001; Raywid, 1995).

In this case study of a remedial school in Cincinnati, we saw how a public school district's office of student discipline facilitated the development of a new form of partnership between teachers and parents of at-risk students. We saw that at Project Succeed Academy in the 1990s, the director of the office of student discipline encouraged teachers and parents to come together to create a more family-like environment in the school, a more school-like environment in students' homes, and a stronger home–school learning community focused more on the needs of at-risk children. To accomplish this task, teachers and parents had to overcome barriers to communication associated with differences in socioeconomic class and ethnic status and to develop consensus on a range of disciplinary policies and educational programs that everyone involved in the school could commit to. We also saw that even after the remedial school was closed and the Project Succeed program came to an end, many of its innovative policies and programs continued in the elementary and middle schools in the district serving large numbers of at-risk students that had adopted specific Project Succeed policies and programs and in the district-wide code of student behavior that had been developed in conjunction with the Project Succeed program.

All schools are intended to serve the communities that create and sustain them. In the suburban and small-town school districts that created the first alternative high schools, White middle-class teachers and White middle-class parents worked together to develop more challenging educational environments for students, who were encouraged to focus on developing their individual gifts and talents (Raywid, 1994b). In the large urban districts that created the first remedial elementary and middle schools, on the other hand, the first task of White middle-class teachers and low-income and ethnic minority parents was to work together to develop a comprehensive and consistent disciplinary environment in which students could focus on developing their academic and social skills. At the same time, all alternative schools are intended to be innovative. The first alternatives were innovative in the areas of school structures and curriculum (Raywid, 1994b); remedial schools were innovative mainly in the areas of student discipline and parent involvement (Carpenter-Aeby & Aeby, 2001). Serving disproportionately large numbers of low-income and ethnic minority students raised in homes with different standards of discipline, remedial schools were required to develop new disciplinary policies, and serving students whose disruptive behavior and poor academic performance in regular schools had their roots in home environments which suffered from the challenges associated with poverty and discrimination, the schools were required to make greater efforts to involve school staff in the home and to involve parents in the school (Dynarski & Gleason, 2002; Fine, 1993).

At Project Succeed Academy, however, innovation was taken one step further. In the process of developing consensus on new disciplinary policies and educational programs for at-risk students, Project Succeed teachers and parents created a school which became the focus for building a stronger home–school learning community. In this new community, as in the earliest alternative schools, parents actively supported teachers and, as in the early remedial schools, teachers actively supported parents. During this collaboration, the focus of everyone's efforts soon became the strengthening of school

Conclusion

itself. When teachers no longer saw the school as being exclusively theirs, rather than asking how parents could support them they asked what parents needed if they were to partner with teachers in the day-to-day activities of the school. At the same time, when parents came to see the school as something they helped create, rather than asking what teachers could do for their children they asked what they had to do to prepare themselves to carry their share of the load. When teachers attended parent nights to share the skills parents would need to extend the work of the school into the home, and when parents volunteered at the school to help create the sort of family-like atmosphere it was often difficult for them to provide at home, teachers and parents were recognizing their shared membership in a larger home–school learning community which would have a more profound and lasting impact on children than anything they could achieve on their own.

The limitations of the present study are obvious. Any case study faces the problem of generalizability, and the present study might be seen to be unique both in terms of its historical context and in the particular group of students, teachers, and parents described. Given these limitations, the study may seem to offer little guidance to future students of urban education confronted with different historical contexts and different groups of students, teachers, and parents. But the new form of home–school community that was found to be effective in one alternative school for at-risk students in Cincinnati in the 1990s is not completely different from the forms of community found in other alternative schools, nor would implementing it in current and future remedial schools for elementary and middle students present insurmountable challenges.

First, urban school districts no longer need external pressure from federal courts, city governments, or business communities to establish remedial schools for at-risk students, and they continue to do so in ever-increasing numbers. All that is needed now is recognition of the fact that no temporary program can be expected to effect the permanent changes in student behavior that are required for at-risk students to succeed. Second, recruiting experienced teachers who have proved themselves effective in teaching at-risk elementary and middle school students is not a major challenge. Most PSA teachers had long wanted to do more for their students, and Project Succeed gave them the opportunity (Henderson-Frye, 1999). Third, involving parents who might be initially hostile to the idea of an alternative school for their children and want to keep their distance from the school is unlikely to prove a major issue. When Cincinnati parents saw their children responding positively to PSA teachers and teachers reaching out to share the PSA program with them, and when they realized that the school required only as much involvement as they were able to give and then offered them all the support they needed to become involved, most parents were willing to participate. If Project Succeed is any guide, success at alternative schools for at-risk elementary and middle school students depends only on school districts creating opportunities for some of their best teachers to do their best work and for some of their most concerned parents to become more involved in more positive ways.

The lead author's primary role in the process of designing, developing, and implementing an alternative school for at-risk elementary and middle school students was similar to a role played by Black principals in separate Black schools during segregation. This is the same role that has been emphasized in research on Black principals in predominantly Black schools today. Creating a summer reading program which reached out to predominantly African American parents and guardians, assisting in establishing a parents association to coordinate the activities of parents and community members, and encouraging the parents to get involved in an initiative for a year-round school—all of this called for a commitment to Black education, an understanding of disruptive Black students, and an ability to communicate with Black parents.

But the lead author also played a second role at the school, a role that was crucial in the development and implementation of a new district-wide code of student behavior. This second role, though also analogous to a role played by Black principals during segregation, is not one that is emphasized in research on Black educational leaders today. Involving African American and urban Appalachian parents at the school and teachers and student case managers in parents' homes; creating a disciplinary advisory board that included disadvantaged parents and wealthy businesspeople and project teams which included representatives from a teachers federation and a Baptist ministers conference, all of which required consensual decision making; and lobbying a majority-White school board to listen to mostly African American parents and encouraging parents to give testimonials to the board—all of this involved facilitating meaningful communication and mediating disagreements between a city's Black and White communities.

In coming to this understanding of the role he played in the reform of an urban school district's student discipline policies and programs, the lead author was aware of the importance of critical race theory's notion of interest convergence. An alternative school for chronically disruptive students would clearly benefit the vast majority of teachers who work in regular schools. Equally clearly, an alternative school based on a successful summer reading program was likely to benefit the children of disadvantaged and minority parents who might otherwise be opposed to alternative forms of education. But if the idea of interest convergence seemed necessary to explain what brought different groups together and the general outcomes of their work, it was not sufficient to account for what actually occurred in the process of developing the alternative school and the district-wide code of student behavior. In the case of the meeting between the executive councils of the teachers federation and the Baptist ministers conference and the two groups' subsequent alliance, for example, what was remarkable was how much more energy and creativity went into the development process after it became clear that their respective interests would be satisfied. Throughout the development process, the lead author witnessed individuals and groups reaching out to each other. Like crusaders for Black education in the 19th century, they could all agree on the ultimate importance of the sanctity of knowledge and the innate humanity of all children and that beneath their obvious differences were areas of substantial agreement that could form the basis for new policies and programs they could commit to personally and advocate for with others.

We have been guided in this study by Dewey's notions of community and communication. But for Dewey community and communication are related to his idea of democracy. Coming of age during the Progressive era, Dewey witnessed first hand the challenges industrialization, immigration, and urbanization presented to urban governments and to urban school systems. He championed progressive educational ideas in part because he saw that traditional public schools were unable to respond to the needs of new student populations. In our own era, characterized by post-industrialization, immigration, and desegregation, the basic challenges remain the same. How are traditionally White middle-class public schools to respond to low-income and ethnic and linguistic minority students?

For urban school districts today one of the most important challenges is to identify educators who can effectively lead increasingly diverse school communities. The problem is that leaders must add to their prior commitment to their own group a new responsibility to facilitate communication between groups. Though this may require new skills, especially linguistic skills, the present study would indicate that a more important requirement is the ability to live with a duality characteristic of African American experience (Fordham, 1996), that is, to hold multiple identities and multiple responsibilities without debilitating conflict. But if the present study is any guide, the solution to this problem is clear: urban school districts must identify as future leaders educators whose first commitment is to the sanctity of knowledge and the innate humanity of all children and who have a proven ability to work with different groups and individuals and to share their vision with them. When teachers enroll in urban educational leadership programs, they typically bring to their studies an intimate knowledge of urban schools which emphasize the importance of community and communication. We hope that engaging this volume will be of some help to these future leaders in reflecting on their experience and in preparing for the time they will be required to help facilitate communication and build community in their schools.

References

Abrams, L. S., & Gibbs, J. T. (2000). Planning for school change: School-community collaboration in a full-service elementary school. *Urban Education*, 35, 79–103.

────── (2002). Disrupting the logic of home-school relations: Parent involvement strategies and practices of inclusion and exclusion. *Urban Education*, 37, 384–407.

Aeby, V. G., Manning, B. H., Thyer, B. A., & Carpenter-Aeby, T. (1999). Comparing outcomes of an alternative school program offered with and without intensive family involvement. *School Community Journal*, 9, 17–32.

America's toughest principal? (1983, April 14). *The Cincinnati Post*, pp. 1A, 7A.

Anyon, J. (1997). *Ghetto schooling: A political economy of urban educational reform*. New York: Teachers College Press.

Armor, D. J. (1995). *Forced justice: School desegregation and the law*. New York: Oxford University Press.

Arnett Ferguson, A. (2000). *Bad boys: Public schools in the making of black masculinity*. Ann Arbor: University of Michigan Press.

Arnold, D. H., Ortiz, C., Curl, J. C., Stowe, R. M., Goldstein, N. F., Fisher, P. H., Zeljo, A., & Yershova, I. (1999). Promoting academic success and preventing disruptive behavior disorders through community partnerships. *Journal of Community Psychology*, 27, 589–598.

Bakari, R. (2003). Preservice teachers' attitudes toward teaching African American students. *Urban Education*, 38, 640–654.

Barton, P. E., Coley, R. J., & Wenglinsky, H. (1998). *Order in the classroom: Violence, discipline, and student achievement*. Princeton, NJ: Education Testing Service.

Beating by police angers Cincinnatians (1995, April 30). *The Dayton Daily News*, p. 1A.

Beauboeuf-Lafontant, T. (1999). A movement against and beyond boundaries: Politically relevant teaching among African American teachers. *Teachers College Record*, 100, 702–723.

Bertaux, N. E. (1994). Exploring the connections among gender, race, and ethnicity in the public schools of 19th century Cincinnati, Ohio. *Humanity & Society*, 18, 37–48.

Bertaux, N., & Washington, M. (2005). The "colored schools" of Cincinnati and African American community in nineteenth-century Cincinnati, 1849–1890. *Journal of Negro Education*, 74, 43–52.

Bloom comes to life (1981, November 16). *The Cincinnati Post*, pp. 1A, 10A.

Borman, K. M., Lippincott, N. T., & Matey, C. M. (1978). Family and classroom control in an urban Appalachian neighborhood. *Education and Urban Society*, 11, 61–86.

Borman, K. M., & Spring, J. H. (1984). *Schools in central cities: Structure and process*. New York: Longman.

Borman, K. M., & Stegelin, D. (1994). Social change and urban Appalachian children: Youth at risk. In K. M. Borman & P. J. Obermiller (Eds.), *From mountain to metropolis: Appalachian migrants in American cities* (pp. 167–180). Westport, CT: Bergin & Garvey.

Boyd-Franklin, N., & Franklin, A. J. (2000). *Boys into men: Raising our African American teenage sons.* New York: Dutton.

Bradley, A. (1994, January 19). The discipline dilemma. *Education Week*, 13, 20–24.

Brown, L. H. (1992). *Discipline advisory board report and recommendations.* Cincinnati, OH: Cincinnati Public Schools Office of Student Discipline.

——— (2004). Project Succeed Academy: A private-public partnership to develop a holistic approach for serving students with behavioral problems. *Urban Education*, 39, 5–32.

——— (2005). America's Black male: Disadvantaged from birth to death. *Perspectives on Urban Education*. Retrieved April 5, 2007, from http://www.urbanedjournal.org/notes/notes0016.htm.

Brown, L. H., & Beckett, K. S. (2006). The role of the school district in student discipline: Building consensus in Cincinnati. *Urban Review*, 38, 235–256.

——— (2007). Building community in an urban school district: A case study of African American educational leadership. *School Community Journal*, 17, 7–32.

——— (In press). Parent involvement in an alternative school for students at risk of educational failure. *Education and Urban Society*.

Brown, L. H., Beckett, G. H., & Beckett K. S. (2006). Segregation, desegregation, and resegregation in Cincinnati: The perspective of an African American principal. *Journal of School Leadership*, 16, 265–291.

Browne, J. A., Losen, D. J., & Wald. J. (2002). Zero tolerance: Unfair, with little recourse. *New Directions for Youth Development*, 92, 73–99.

Bryant, N. (1998). Reducing the relational distance between actors: A case study in school reform. *Urban Education*, 33, 34–49.

Buenger, C. L. (1991). *Report and recommendations of the task force on public schools.* Cincinnati, OH: Cincinnati Business Committee.

Butchart, R. E. (1990). Recruits to the "army of civilization": Gender, race, class, and the freedmen's teachers, 1862–1875. *Journal of Education*, 172, 76–87.

Calabrese, R. L. (1990). The public school: A source of alienation for minority parents. *Journal of Negro Education*, 59, 148–154.

Carpenter-Aeby, T., & Aeby, V. G. (2001). Family-school-community interventions for chronically disruptive students: An evaluation of outcomes in an alternative school. *School Community Journal*, 11, 75–92.

Case, K. I. (1997). African American othermothering in the urban elementary school. *The Urban Review*, 29, 25–39.

Christle, C., Nelson, C. M., & Jolivette, K. (2004). School characteristics related to the use of suspension. *Education and Treatment of Children*, 27, 509–526.

Clark, M. D. (1993, November 18). Teachers union solicits Baptist ministers' help. *The Cincinnati Post*, p. 12A.

——— (1995, November 11). New school for unruly kids a step closer. *The Cincinnati Post*, p. 1A.

References

Clotfelter, C. T. (2004). *After* Brown*: The rise and retreat of school desegregation*. Princeton, NJ: Princeton University Press.

Comer, J. P. (1997). *Waiting for a miracle: Why schools can't solve our problems—and how we can*. New York: Dutton.

Cook, D. A., & Fine, M. (1995). "Motherwit": Childrearing lessons from African-American mothers of low income. In B. B. Swadener & S. Lubeck (Eds.), *Children and families "at promise": Deconstructing the discourse of risk* (pp. 118–142). Albany: State University of New York Press.

Cooper, R., & Jordan, W. J. (2003). Cultural issues in comprehensive school reform. *Urban Education*, 38, 380–397.

Cox, S. M., Davidson, W. S., & Bynum, T. S. (1995). A meta-analytic assessment of delinquency-related outcomes of alternative education programs. *Crime & Delinquency*, 41, 219–234.

Crowley, M. R. (1938). Cincinnati's experiment in Negro education: A comparative study of the segregated and mixed schools. *Journal of Negro Education*, 1, 25–33.

Crozier, G. (1999). Is it a case of "We know when we're not wanted"? The parents' perspective on parent-teacher roles and relationships. *Educational Research*, 41, 315–328.

——— (2000). *Parents and schools: Partners or antagonists?* Sterling, VA: Trentham.

Cullingford, C., & Morrison, M. (1999). Relationships between parents and schools: A case study. *Educational Review*, 51, 253–262.

Dauber, S. L., & Epstein, J. L. (1993). Parents' attitudes and practices of involvement in inner city elementary and middle schools. In N. F. Chavkin (Ed.), *Families and schools in a pluralistic society* (pp. 53–71). Albany: State University of New York Press.

Davis, J. E. (2001). Black boys at school: Negotiating masculinities and race. In R. Majors (Ed.), *Educating our Black children: New directions and radical approaches* (pp. 169–182). New York: RoutledgeFalmer.

——— (2003). Early schooling and academic achievement of African American males. *Urban Education*, 38, 515–537.

Dempsey, V., & Noblit, G. (1993a). The demise of caring in an African American community: One consequence of school desegregation. *The Urban Review*, 25, 47–61.

——— (1993b). Cultural ignorance and school desegregation: Reconstructing a silenced narrative. *Educational Policy*, 7, 318–339.

Dewey, J. (1916/1944). *Democracy and education: An introduction to the philosophy of education*. New York: The Free Press.

Diamond, J. B., & Gomez, K. (2004). African American parents' educational orientations: The importance of social class and parents' perceptions of schools. *Education and Urban Society*, 36, 383–427.

Dillard, C. B. (1995). Leading with her life: An African American feminist (re)interpretation of leadership for an urban high school principal. *Educational Administration Quarterly*, 31, 539–563.

Dimond, P. R. (1985). *Beyond busing: Inside the challenge to urban desegregation*. Ann Arbor: University of Michigan Press.

Discipline in city schools (1993, April 2). *The Cincinnati Post*, p. 10a.

Downey, D. B., & Pribesh, S. (2004). When race matters: Teachers' evaluations of students' classroom behavior. *Sociology of Education*, 77, 267–282.

Dunbar, C., Jr. (1999). African American males and participation: Promising inclusion, practicing exclusion. *Theory into Practice*, 38, 241–246.

——— (2001). *Alternative schooling for African American youth: Does anyone know we're here?* New York: Peter Lang.

Dynarski, M., & Gleason, P. (2002). How can we help? What we have learned from recent federal dropout prevention evaluations. *Journal of Education for Students Placed at Risk*, 7, 43–69.

Erkins, E. K. (2002). A case study of desegregation in Cincinnati public schools: 1974 to 1994. Unpublished doctoral dissertation, University of Cincinnati.

Fairclough, A. (2001). *Teaching equality: Black schools in the age of Jim Crow*. Athens: University of Georgia Press.

Farkas, S., & Johnson, J. (1998). *Time to move on: African American and White parents set an agenda for public schools*. New York: Public Agenda.

Fields-Smith, C. (2005). African American parents before and after *Brown*. *Journal of Curriculum and Supervision*, 20, 129–135.

Fine, M. (1993). [Ap]parent involvement: Reflections on parents, power, and urban public schools. *Teachers College Record*, 94, 682–710.

——— (1995). The politics of who's "at risk." In B. B. Swadener & S. Lubeck (Eds.), *Children and families "at promise": Deconstructing the discourse of risk* (pp. 76–94). Albany: State University of New York Press.

Fordham, S. (1996). *Blacked out: Dilemmas of race, identity, and success at Capital High*. Chicago, IL: University of Chicago Press.

——— (2001). Why can't Sonya (and Kwame) fail math? In W. H. Watkins, J. H. Lewis, & V. Chou (Eds.), *Race and education: The roles of history and society in educating African American students* (pp. 140–158). Boston, MA: Allyn and Bacon.

Foster, M. (1990). The politics of race: Through the eyes of African-American teachers. *Journal of Education*, 172, 123–141.

——— (1993). Educating for competence in community and culture: Exploring the views of exemplary African-American teachers. *Urban Education*, 27, 370–394.

——— (1997). *Black teachers on teaching*. New York: New Press.

Foster, M., & Peele, T. B. (1999). Teaching Black males: Lessons from the experts. In V. C. Polite & J. E. Davis (Eds.), *African American males in school and society: Practices and policies for effective education* (pp. 8–19). New York: Teachers College Press.

Franklin, V. P. (1990). "They rose and fell together": African American educators and community leadership, 1795–1954. *Journal of Education*, 172, 39–64.

Furlong, A. (2005). Cultural dimensions of decisions about educational participation among 14- to 19-year-olds: The parts that Tomlinson doesn't reach. *Journal of Education Policy*, 20, 379–389.

Garvin Fields, M. (1983). *Lemon Swamp and other places: A Carolina memoir*. New York: The Free Press.

Gentry, A. A., & Peelle, C. C. (1994). *Learning to survive: Black youth look for education and hope*. Westport, CT: Auburn House.

References

George, H. P., Harrower, J. K., & Knoster, T. (2003). School-wide prevention and early intervention: A process for establishing a system of school-wide behavior support. *Preventing School Failure*, 47, 170–176.

Gerber, D. A. (1973). Education, expediency, and ideology: Race and politics in the desegregation of Ohio public schools in the late 19th century. *Journal of Ethnic Studies*, 1(3), 1–31.

Gold, M., & Mann, D. W. (1984). *Expelled to a friendlier place: A study of effective alternative schools.* Ann Arbor: University of Michigan Press.

Goldring, E., & Smrekar, C. (2000). Magnet schools and the pursuit of racial balance. *Education and Urban Society*, 33, 17–35.

Gooden, M. A. (2005). The role of an African American principal in an urban information technology high school. *Educational Administration Quarterly*, 41, 630–650.

Goodman, G. S. (1999). *Alternatives in education: Critical pedagogy for disaffected youth.* New York: Peter Lang.

Gordon, J. A. (1998). Caring through control: Reaching urban African American youth. *Journal for a Just and Caring Education*, 4, 418–440.

Gottfredson, D. C. (1997). School-based crime prevention. In L. W. Sherman, D. C. Gottfredson, D. MacKenzie, J. Eck, P. Reuter, & S. Bushway (Eds.), *Preventing crime: What works, what doesn't, what's promising: A report to the United States Congress.* Washington, DC: U.S. Department of Justice Office of Justice Programs.

—— (2001). *Schools and delinquency.* Cambridge, UK: Cambridge University Press.

Gouldner, H. (1978). *Teachers' pets, troublemakers, and nobodies: Black children in elementary school.* Westport, CT: Greenwood.

Griggs, F. (1998, June 4). Experimental school finds discipline problems deeply rooted. *The Cincinnati Post*. Retrieved September 15, 2006, from http://www.cincypost.com/news/1998/succ060498.html.

Hale-Benson, J. (1989). The school learning environment and academic success. In G. L. Berry & J. K. Asamen (Eds.), *Black students: Psychosocial issues and academic achievement* (pp. 83–97). Newbury Park, CA: Sage.

Henderson-Frye, D. L. (1999). *At-risk students at promise: A case study of a middle school program that facilitates the promise of children at risk.* Unpublished doctoral dissertation, University of Cincinnati.

Hess, F. M., & Leal, D. L. (2001). The opportunity to engage: How race, class, and institutions structure access to educational deliberation. *Educational Policy*, 15, 474–490.

Holzman, M. (2004). *Public education and Black male students: A state report card. Schott Educational Inequity Index.* Cambridge, MA: Schott Foundation for Public Education.

Howard, T. C. (2001). Telling their side of the story: African-American students' perceptions of culturally relevant teaching. *Urban Review*, 33, 131–149.

—— (2002). Hearing footsteps in the dark: African American students' descriptions of effective teachers. *Journal of Education for Students Placed at Risk*, 7, 425–444.

Hughes, J. N., Gleason, K. A., & Zhang, D. (2005). Relationship influences on teachers' perceptions of academic competence in academically at-risk minority and majority first grade students. *Journal of School Psychology*, 43, 303–320.

Hull, J. D. (1994, April 4). Do teachers punish according to race? *Time*. Retrieved April 5, 2007, from http://www.time.com/time/magazine/article/0,9171,980428,00.html?promoid=googlep.
Junious Williams, J. D. (1993). Study of racial disparities in student suspensions in the Cincinnati, Ohio, school district. Oakland, CA: Urban Strategies Council.
Kelly, D. M. (1993). *Last Chance High: How girls and boys drop in and out of alternative schools*. New Haven, CT: Yale University Press.
Kennedy, R. L., & Morton, J. H. (1999). *A school for healing: Alternative strategies for teaching at-risk students*. New York: Peter Lang.
Kleiner, B., Porch, R., & Farris, E. (2002). *Public alternative schools and programs for students at risk of education failure: 2000–01* (NCES 2002-004). Washington, DC: U.S. Department of Education National Center for Education Statistics.
Kunjufu, J. (1986). *Countering the conspiracy to destroy black boys*. Vol. II. Chicago, IL: African American Images.
Ladson-Billings, G. (1999). Just what is critical race theory in educational research and praxis? In L. Parker, D. Deyhle, & S. Villenas (Eds.), *Race is ... race isn't: Critical race theory and qualitative studies in education* (pp. 7–30). Boulder, CO: Westview.
Ladson-Billings, G., & Tate, W. F., IV (1995). Toward a critical race theory of education. *Teachers College Record*, 97, 47–68.
Lareau, A. (1987). Social class differences in family-school relationships: The importance of cultural capital. *Sociology of Education*, 60, 73–85.
——— (1996). Assessing parent involvement in school: A critical analysis. In A. Booth & J. F. Dunn (Eds.), *Family-school links: How do they affect educational outcomes?* (pp. 57–64). Mahwah, NJ: Lawrence Erlbaum.
——— (2000). *Home advantage: Social class and parental intervention in elementary education*. 2nd Ed.. New York: Rowman & Littlefield.
Lareau, A., & Horvat, E. M. (1999). Moments of social inclusion and exclusion: Race, class, and cultural capital in family-school relationships. *Sociology of Education*, 72, 37–53.
Lasley, T. J., & Wayson, W. W. (1982). Characteristics of schools with good discipline. *Educational Leadership*, 40(3), 28–31.
Lehr, C. A., & Lange, C. M. (2003). Alternative schools serving students with and without disabilities: What are the current issues and challenges? *Preventing School Failure*, 47, 59–65.
Lei, J. L. (2003). (Un)necessary toughness?: Those "loud Black girls" and those "quiet Asian boys." *Anthropology and Education Quarterly*, 34, 158–181.
Lomotey, K. (1989). *African-American principals: School leadership and success*. New York: Greenwood.
——— (1990). Qualities shared by African-American principals in effective schools: A preliminary analysis. In K. Lomotey (Ed.), *Going to school: The African-American experience* (pp. 197–207). Albany: State University of New York Press.
McGee, J. (2001). Reflections of an alternative school administrator. *Phi Delta Kappan*, 82, 588–591.
Miretzky, D. (2004). The communication requirements of democratic schools: Parent-teacher perspectives on their relationships. *Teachers College Record*, 106, 814–851.

References

Moles, O. C. (1993). Collaboration between schools and disadvantaged parents: Obstacles and openings. In N. F. Chavkin (Ed.), *Families and schools in a pluralistic society* (pp. 21–49). Albany: State University of New York Press.

Monroe, C. R., & Obidah, J. E. (2004). The influence of cultural synchronization on a teacher's perceptions of disruption: A case study of an African American middle-school classroom. *Journal of Teacher Education*, 55, 256–268.

Morris, J. E. (1999). A pillar of strength: An African American school's communal bonds with families and community since *Brown*. *Urban Education*, 33, 584–605.

——— (2004). Can anything good come from Nazareth? Race, class, and African American schooling and community in the urban South and Midwest. *American Educational Research Journal*, 41, 69–112.

Murrell, P. C., Jr. (2002). *African-centered pedagogy: Developing schools of achievement for African American children*. Albany: State University of New York Press.

Murtadhu-Watts, K. (2000). Theorizing urban black masculinity construction in an African-centered school. In N. Lesko (Ed.), *Masculinities at school* (pp. 49–71). Thousand Oaks, CA: Sage.

National Center for Education Statistics (2005). National Assessment of Educational Progress: Long term trend. Retrieved August 28, 2005, from http://nces.ed.gov/nationsreportcard/ltt/results2004/natsubgroups.asp.

Nearing, S. (1915/1969). *The new education*. New York: Arno Press & The New York Times.

Noguera, P. A. (2003). Schools, prisons, and social implications of punishment: Rethinking disciplinary practices. *Theory into Practice*, 42, 341–350.

Nolen, C. H. (2001). *African American southerners in slavery, Civil War and Reconstruction*. Jefferson, NC: McFarland & Company.

Obermiller, P. J., Borman, K. M., & Kroger, J. A. (1988). The Lower Price Hill community school: Strategies for social change from an Appalachian street academy. *Urban Education*, 23, 123–132.

O'Connor, S. (2001). Voices of parents and teachers in a poor white urban school. *Journal of Education for Students Placed at Risk*, 6, 175–198.

Ogbu, J. U. (2003). *Black American students in an affluent suburb: A study of academic disengagement*. Mahwah, NJ: Lawrence Erlbaum.

Penn, E. M., Borman, K. M., & Hoeweler, F. (1994). Echoes from the hill: Urban Appalachian youths and educational reform. In K. M. Borman & P. J. Obermiller (Eds.), *From mountain to metropolis: Appalachian migrants in American cities* (pp. 121–140). Westport, CT: Bergin & Garvey.

Principal gets firm grip on Withrow (1986, October 21). *The Cincinnati Post*, p. 1A.

Project Succeed Academy: A smart program (1996, August 22). *The Cincinnati Post*, p. 20A.

Pugh-Lilly, A. O., Neville, H. A., & Poulin, K. L. (2001). In protection of ourselves: Black girls' perceptions of self-reported delinquent behavior. *Psychology of Women Quarterly*, 25, 145–154.

Queenan, B. (1998, September 25). From attention deficit to discipline: Martial arts help ADD children to concentrate. *The Cincinnati Post*, p. 1B.

Raffaele Mendez, L. M., Knoff, H. M., & Ferron, J. M. (2002). School demographic variables and out-of-school suspension rates: A quantitative and qualitative analysis of a large, ethnically diverse school district. *Psychology in the Schools*, 39, 259–277.

Raywid, M. A. (1993). Community: An alternative school accomplishment. In G. A. Smith (Ed.), *Public schools that work: Creating community* (pp. 23–44). New York: Routledge.

——— (1994a). A school that really works: Urban Academy. *Journal of Negro Education*, 63, 93–110.

——— (1994b). Alternative schools: The state of the art. *Educational Leadership*, 52 (September 1994), 26–31.

——— (1994c). Synthesis of research on schools of choice. In J. Kretovics & E. J. Nussel (Eds.), *Transforming urban education* (pp. 214–227). Boston, MA: Allyn and Bacon.

——— (1995). Alternatives and marginal students. In M. C. Wang & M. C. Reynolds (Eds.), *Making a difference for students at risk: Trends and alternatives* (pp. 119–155). Thousand Oaks, CA: Corwin.

Reitzug, U. C., & Patterson, J. (1998). "I'm not going to lose you!" Empowerment through caring in an urban principal's practice with students. *Urban Education*, 33, 150–181.

Rist, R. C. (1973/2002). *The urban school: A factory for failure*. Cambridge, MA: MIT Press.

Scates, D. E. (1938). Cincinnati colored teachers set a standard. *Journal of Negro Education*, 7, 144–146.

Schutz, A., & Harris, I. M. (2001). The fragility of community and function: A snapshot of an alternative school in crisis. *Encounter*, 14, 39–53.

Schwartz, W. (2001). *School practices for equitable discipline of African American students*. New York: Eric Clearinghouse on Urban Education.

Scott, T. M., Nelson, C. M., & Liaupsin, C. J. (2001). Effective instruction: The forgotten component in preventing school violence. *Education & Treatment of Children*, 24, 309–322.

Sekou Collins, P. K. (2004). The roof is on fire: Doing historical archeology on 19th-century education in a city in turmoil. *Journal of Black Studies*, 35, 23–39.

Sheldon, S. B., & Epstein, J. L. (2002). Improving student behavior and school discipline with family and community involvement. *Education and Urban Society*, 35, 4–26.

Siddle Walker, V. (1993). Interpersonal caring in the "good" segregated schooling of African-American children: Evidence from the case of Caswell County Training School. *Urban Review*, 25, 63–77.

——— (1996). *Their highest potential: An African American school community in the segregated South*. Chapel Hill: University of North Carolina Press.

——— (2000). Valued segregated schools for African American children in the South, 1935–1969: A review of common themes and characteristics. *Review of Educational Research*, 70, 253–285.

——— (2003). The architects of Black schooling in the segregated South: The case of one principal leader. *Journal of Curriculum and Supervision*, 19, 54–72.

Skiba, R. (2001). When is disproportionality discrimination? The overrepresentation of Black students in school suspension. In W. Ayers, B. Dohrn, & R. Ayers (Eds.), *Zero tolerance: Resisting the drive for punishment in our schools: A handbook for parents, students, educators, and citizens* (pp. 176–187). New York: The New Press.

References

Skiba, R. J., & Knesting, K. (2001). Zero tolerance, zero evidence: An analysis of school disciplinary practice, *New Directions for Youth Development*, 92, 17–43.

Skiba, R. J., Michael, R. S., Nardo, A. C., & Peterson, R. L. (2002). The color of discipline: Sources of racial and gender disproportionality in administration of school punishment. *The Urban Review*, 34, 317–342.

Smrekar, C., & Cohen-Vogel, L. (2001). The voices of parents: Rethinking the intersection of family and school. *Peabody Journal of Education*, 76, 75–100.

Smrekar, C., & Goldring, E. (1999). *School choice in urban America: Magnet schools and the pursuit of equity*. New York: Teachers College Press.

Spring, J. (1994). *The American school: 1642–1993*. 3rd Ed. New York: McGraw-Hill.

——— (2005). *The American school: 1642–2004*. 6th Ed. Boston: McGraw-Hill.

Stanford, G. C. (1998). African-American teachers' knowledge of teaching: Understanding the influence of their remembered teachers. *Urban Review*, 30, 229–243.

Swadener, B. B., & Lubeck S. (Eds.) (1995). *Children and families "at promise": Deconstructing the discourse of risk*. Albany: State University of New York Press.

Swaminathan, R. (2004). "It's my place": Student perspectives on urban school effectiveness. *School Effectiveness and School Improvement*, 15, 33–63.

Taylor, W. L., & Yu, C. M. (1999). The context of magnet schools: The policies and politics of desegregation in Cincinnati and St. Louis. In C. Smrekar & E. Goldring, *School choice in urban America: Magnet schools and the pursuit of equity* (pp. 15–25). New York: Teachers College Press.

Thompson, G. L. (2002). *African American teens discuss their schooling experiences*. Westport, CT: Bergin & Garvey.

Top award for Project Succeed. (1997, April 25). *The Cincinnati Post*, p. 14A.

Townsend, B. L. (2000). The disproportionate discipline of African American learners: Reducing school suspensions and expulsions. *Exceptional Children*, 66, 381–391.

Tyack, D. B. (1974). *The one best system: A history of American urban education*. Cambridge, MA: Harvard University Press.

Tyack, D., & Hansot, E. (1982). *Managers of virtue: Public school leadership in America, 1820–1980*. New York: Basic Books.

Tyson, K. (2003). Notes from the back of the room: Problems and paradoxes in the schooling of young black students. *Sociology of Education*, 76, 326–343.

Vaden-Kiernan, N., & McManus, J. (2005). *Parent and family involvement in education: 2002–03* (NCES 2005-043). Washington, DC: U.S. Department of Education National Center for Education Statistics.

Vavrus, F., & Cole, K. (2002). "I didn't do nothin'": The discursive construction of school suspension. *Urban Review*, 34, 87–111.

Washington, M. H. (1984). The Black struggle for desegregated quality education: Cincinnati, Ohio 1942–1974. Unpublished doctoral thesis, University of Cincinnati.

Watras, J. (1997). *Politics, race, and schools: Racial integration, 1954–1994*. New York: Garland.

Weininger, E. B., & Lareau, A. (2003). Translating Bourdieu into the American context: The question of social class and family-school relations. *Poetics*, 31, 375–402.

Whitman, M. (1998). *The irony of desegregation law*. Princeton, NJ: Markus Wiener.

Wiest, D. J., Wong, E. H., Cervantes, L. C., & Kreil, D. A. (2001). Intrinsic motivation among regular, special, and alternative education high school students. *Adolescence*, 36, 111–126.

Studies in the Postmodern Theory of Education

General Editors
Joe L. Kincheloe & Shirley R. Steinberg

Counterpoints publishes the most compelling and imaginative books being written in education today. Grounded on the theoretical advances in criticism, feminism, and postmodernism in the last two decades of the twentieth century, Counterpoints engages the meaning of these innovations in various forms of educational expression. Committed to the proposition that theoretical literature should be accessible to a variety of audiences, the series insists that its authors avoid esoteric and jargonistic languages that transform educational scholarship into an elite discourse for the initiated. Scholarly work matters only to the degree it affects consciousness and practice at multiple sites. Counterpoints' editorial policy is based on these principles and the ability of scholars to break new ground, to open new conversations, to go where educators have never gone before.

For additional information about this series or for the submission of manuscripts, please contact:

> Joe L. Kincheloe & Shirley R. Steinberg
> c/o Peter Lang Publishing, Inc.
> 29 Broadway, 18th floor
> New York, New York 10006

To order other books in this series, please contact our Customer Service Department:

> (800) 770-LANG (within the U.S.)
> (212) 647-7706 (outside the U.S.)
> (212) 647-7707 FAX

Or browse online by series:
> www.peterlang.com